Stories of Progressive Institutional Change

Deborah M. Figart

Stories of Progressive Institutional Change

Challenges to the Neoliberal Economy

Deborah M. Figart
Stockton University
Galloway, NJ
USA

ISBN 978-3-319-59778-2   ISBN 978-3-319-59779-9   (eBook)
DOI 10.1007/978-3-319-59779-9

Library of Congress Control Number: 2017943809

© The Editor(s) (if applicable) and The Author(s) 2017
This work is subject to copyright. All rights are solely and exclusively licensed by the Publisher, whether the whole or part of the material is concerned, specifically the rights of translation, reprinting, reuse of illustrations, recitation, broadcasting, reproduction on microfilms or in any other physical way, and transmission or information storage and retrieval, electronic adaptation, computer software, or by similar or dissimilar methodology now known or hereafter developed.
The use of general descriptive names, registered names, trademarks, service marks, etc. in this publication does not imply, even in the absence of a specific statement, that such names are exempt from the relevant protective laws and regulations and therefore free for general use.
The publisher, the authors and the editors are safe to assume that the advice and information in this book are believed to be true and accurate at the date of publication. Neither the publisher nor the authors or the editors give a warranty, express or implied, with respect to the material contained herein or for any errors or omissions that may have been made. The publisher remains neutral with regard to jurisdictional claims in published maps and institutional affiliations.

Cover illustration: J555© Harvey Loake

Printed on acid-free paper

This Palgrave Macmillan imprint is published by Springer Nature
The registered company is Springer International Publishing AG
The registered company address is: Gewerbestrasse 11, 6330 Cham, Switzerland

This book is dedicated to progressive change agents and resisters everywhere.

Contents

1 Introduction to Institutions, Institutional Change, and the Stories — 1

2 Accounting for Household Production: Toward an Improved Measure of Macroeconomic Well-Being — 15

3 Funding Infrastructure and Local Economic Development: A Public Bank Option — 27

4 Contesting the Gig Economy: #SchedulesThatWork — 43

5 Delving into the Food Supply Chain: The Case of Fresh Tomatoes — 59

6 Doing Business Responsibly: ROC United and Restaurant Workers — 69

7 Swimming in Debt: Student Loans and the Fight to Save a Generation — 81

8 Transforming Legal Rights and Social Values:
   Marriage Redefined   99

9 Greening the Economy: Certified Sustainable Coffee   113

Index   131

Abbreviations

ABS	Australian Bureau of Statistics
ACLU	American Civil Liberties Union
AFEE	Association for Evolutionary Economics
ALS	Amyotrophic Lateral Sclerosis
ASCE	American Society of Civil Engineers
ASSA	Allied Social Sciences Association
ATUS	American Time Use Survey
BEA	Bureau of Economic Analysis
BLS	Bureau of Labor Statistics
BND	Bank of North Dakota
C.A.F.E.	Coffee and Farmer Equity
CEO	Chief Executive Officer
CFPB	Consumer Finance Protection Bureau
CIW	Coalition of Immokalee Workers
CNSTAT	Committee on National Statistics
CPI-U	Consumer Price Index
CWS	Contingent Work Supplement
DADT	"Don't Ask, Don't Tell"
DOMA	Defense of Marriage Act
ENDA	Employment Non-Discrimination Act
EU	European Union
FAO	Food and Agricultural Organization
FDIC	Federal Deposit Insurance Corporation
FINRA	Financial Investor Education Foundation
FLO	Fairtrade International
FLSA	Fair Labor Standards Act
GAO	Government Accountability Office

GDP	Gross Domestic Product
GLAD	Gay & Lesbian Advocates and Defenders
GPA	Grade Point Average
GSL	Guaranteed Student Loan
HEA	Higher Education Act
HRC	Human Rights Campaign
ICA	International Coffee Agreement
IPM	Integrated Pest Management
ITC	International Trade Centre
JwJ	Jobs with Justice
LGBT	Lesbian, Gay, Bisexual, and Transgender
LIAC	Local Investment Advisory Committee
NAS/NRC	National Academy of Sciences/National Research Council
NAWS	National Agriculture Workers Survey
NGOs	Non-Governmental Organizations
NIPA	National Income and Product Accounts
NM	New Mexico
NPL	Nonpartisan League
OECD	Organisation for Economic Co-operation and Development
OIE	Original Institutional Economics
PACE	Partnership in Assisting Community Expansion
PBI	Public Banking Institute
PLUS	Parent Loan for Undergraduate Students
RA	Rainforest Alliance
RAP	Retail Action Project
ROC	Restaurant Opportunities Center United
RWDSU	Retail, Wholesale and Department Store Union
SAN	Sustainable Agriculture Network
SAP	Structural Adjustment Policies
SBA	Small Business Administration
SLAP	Student Labor Action Project
SMBC	Smithsonian Migratory Bird Center
UFCW	United Food and Commercial Workers
UFW	United Farm Workers
UN	United Nations
USSA	United States Student Association
VEDA	Vermont Economic Development Association

List of Figures

Fig. 7.1　Annual percentage change in inflation-adjusted per-student state funding for higher education and in tuition and fees at Public Institutions, 1984–1985 to 2014–2015　　86

List of Tables

Table 8.1 US states with marriage equality through legislation or ballot initiative   107

CHAPTER 1

Introduction to Institutions, Institutional Change, and the Stories

Abstract Progressive institutional change places human, environmental, financial, and productive sustainability at the center of economic processes. To provide a theoretical context, this introductory chapter addresses three questions: (1) What do institutional economists mean by *institutions* and why do they matter in understanding economic life? (2) How do institutional economists explain the evolutionary process of social *change*? and (3) What are the criteria for describing an institutional change as *progressive* instead of regressive? There are multiple avenues for forging institutional change: policies, laws, cultural norms, social movements, and social practices. As the book's eight stories demonstrate, groups are transforming government statistical practice, financial institutions, corporations and their treatment of workers and students, the supply chain for tomatoes, the global market for coffee beans, and civil marriage.

Keywords Institutional economics · Neoliberalism · Economic justice Social movements

JEL Codes B52 · B54 · E02 · Z1

I am intrigued by and inspired by institutional change. I became an economist because of my passion for public policy, specifically efforts to increase economic well-being. Over my career, I have had the opportunity to examine various efforts to effect reform. I have analyzed job quality, discrimination, pay equity, minimum and living wage movements, working time, financial capabilities, and other projects to raise living standards. This intellectual engagement dovetails nicely with my identity as an institutional economist. Institutional economics, along with social economics and feminist economics, has provided me with a framework to both analyze and propose new approaches to organizing economic life. It is because of this interest in change—specifically, institutional change—and its policy relevance, that I was drawn to developing this book.

The idea for this project came out of my work with the Association for Evolutionary Economics (AFEE), a professional association for economists and other social scientists "devoted to analysis of economies as evolving, socially constructed and politically governed systems" (AFEE n.d.). AFEE members draw upon the theoretical school of economics referred to as Original Institutional Economics, based on the work of Thorstein Veblen, John R. Commons, and others. As President-Elect of AFEE in 2015, it was my job to propose a theme for the AFEE-sponsored sessions at the major annual economics conference in North America, the Allied Social Sciences Association annual meetings; I selected "Inside Institutions."

Economic institutions include organizations such as firms, households, community and volunteer groups, and governance institutions. They also include more informal arrangements and interactions among people, as will be elaborated below. The conference theme was designed to encourage participating scholars to examine how institutions evolve and the role of human agency in transforming them. I revisited this theme the following year with my outgoing AFEE presidential address, selecting three institutions undergoing progressive change and sharing short stories about the process. Those stories blossomed into this book, as I saw change in other economic, social, and cultural institutions I wished to investigate, and found more stories to tell.

In my view, this book is both timely and important, especially with the election of US President Donald J. Trump. The antidote to Trump has been activism and resistance. While many of these efforts have necessarily been ad hoc and defensive, there are also ongoing organized movements to effect progressive institutional change, not just in the USA but globally. The chapters in *Stories of Progressive Institutional Change: Challenges to the Neoliberal Economy* highlight sustained activism around valuing caring, ending discrimination, protecting the environment, improving worker well-being, and reimagining ways to encourage local economic development by restoring public–private social balance. They provide examples of how social actors engage in collective behavior in order to advance the objectives of economic justice, democratic participation in economic life, and human development. In order to provide a context for these stories, this chapter addresses three questions to help the reader understand what constitutes progressive institutional change: (1) What do institutional economists mean by *institutions* and why do they matter in understanding economic life? (2) How do institutional economists explain the evolutionary process of social *change*? and (3) What are the criteria for describing an institutional change as *progressive* instead of regressive?

There is certainly no uniformity as to the meaning of institutions (see Alesina and Giuliano 2015; Bromley 2016). In fact, John R. Commons opened an article on institutional economics with the following statement: "The difficulty in defining a field for the so-called institutional economics is the uncertainty of meaning of an institution" (1931, 648). In general though, the various definitions of institutions draw upon economist Thorstein Veblen's concept that human behavior is often habitual, shaped by the society and culture within which a person lives. To Dale Bush, "an 'institution' may be defined as *a set of socially prescribed patterns of correlated behavior*" (1987, 1076, emphasis original). Anne Mayhew broadens her definition to incorporate the meaning behind the behavior, describing institutions as "regular patterns of human activity and their attendant norms, folkviews, understandings and justifications" (2009, 276). Geoffrey Hodgson defines "*institutions* as systems of established and prevalent social rules that structure social interactions" (2006, 2, emphasis original). He argues that institutions both constrain and enable behavior. A behavior becomes an institution—becomes institutionalized—when it is characterized by a degree of rigidity. It becomes normalized and socially expected. However, because institutions are embedded within a particular culture and reflect its norms and values, they can vary greatly.

According to these definitions, laws, accepted systems and customs, as well as firms and organizations are all institutions. Money is an institution because it derives its value from its social context. Shaking hands to cement a business arrangement is an institutionalized pattern of behavior in some societies, but violates social norms in others. Language is an institution, one that relies not only upon a degree of rigidity for mutual understanding but also evolves new words and definitions through the creative activity of the people who use it.

Even some of the common building blocks of economic theory are socially created institutions. The practice of exchanging goods and services for money in a market economy is an institution, for example. Markets are a distinct behavior in modern society, unlike the economic practices in tribal societies where resources were shared among kin, or subsistence economies where most of one's livelihood is self-provisioned. Waged labor is an institution that only evolved with the rise of capitalism, gradually replacing slavery, serfdom, and other labor systems in many parts of the world.

Economists who place the study of institutions at the center of economic life are thus more focused on understanding the context that explains the details of human behavior than in uncovering any universal laws of human behavior. Even the "law of demand"—the idea that people will be more willing and able to purchase something when the price is lower—would not be viewed as a universal truth. Instead, it is understood to be a pattern of behavior that makes sense within a particular social context. Economics is the study of those institutions that shape the process of *social provisioning*, that is, the process of providing for the material needs of community members (Dugger 1996; Waller 2006).

While institutions have some rigidity, they are also continuously evolving. According to Marc Tool and Dale Bush, "[P]erhaps *the* diagnostic characteristic of institutional economics is its focus on the process of institutional change" (2003, xiv, emphasis original; see also Bush 1987). Because institutions are the building blocks of the economy, any theory of economic change must address how institutions evolve over time. Even Nobel laureate Douglass North (2005), a proponent of the "new institutionalism" that synthesizes Original Institutional Economics with neoclassical economic theory, argues that understanding the process of economic change requires studying the dynamics of institutional change (see also Caballero and Soto-Oñate 2015). Such change can be prompted by external shocks or internal contradictions (see Mahoney and Thelen 2009).[1] Specifically, a discrepancy between a group's social values and their prevailing institutional context can generate tensions that instigate a process of institutional change (Dolfsma and Verburg 2008), or change can result from a change in social values themselves.

Finally, institutions influence the distribution of power, so conflict over access to power may motivate social change (Wilber and Harrison 1978, 71).

Understanding institutional change requires peeling back the façade and looking within institutions. Institutions are not economic actors; they do not possess a unitary set of interests. They are created and recreated by groups of people whose interests are sometimes harmonious and sometimes in conflict. Collective behavior is thus the means for changing institutions (Mayhew 2009). Outcomes are not predetermined, nor do they tend toward an optimal or equilibrium point. Rather, as Veblen insisted, we can better understand changes over time using the phrases "blind drift" and "opaque" to indicate that history is non-teleological, or not unfolding toward a specific end (Dugger 1989; Waller 2017).

This means that institutional change is not necessarily "progressive," even if we agree on the meaning of progressive, as opposed to regressive, institutional change. The founders of institutional economics were frequently also advocates of social reform and saw their descriptive analyses of economic life as furthering that end. Yet they wrestled with the ethical basis for making normative claims, due to institutionalism's emphasis on non-determinist historical change and the malleability of human nature. Universal ethical standards are suspect. As a result, some versions of institutionalism run the risk of cultural relativism, accepting the outcomes of any society as representing its own ethical norms without judgment (Mayhew 2009). Such approaches downplay the problem of false consciousness, a crucial concept in Marxian theories of institutional change.

On the other hand, those radical institutional economists who attempt to reconcile the methodologies of institutionalism with Marxism assert that there are broad principles that can be used to categorize institutional change. These principles are grounded in the pragmatic problem solving that has long motivated economists in the institutional tradition. As noted by William Waller, "A successful society is one that uses culturally constructed knowledge to solve its problems of provisioning and sustaining the culture" (2006, 13). Progressive institutional change places long-term thinking—that is, human, environmental, financial, and productive sustainability—at the center of economic processes. Radical institutionalism embraces equality and democracy as core values to promote sustainability and human development (Dugger 1989).

Veblen distinguished between instrumental economic practices that are useful and ceremonial economic practices that merely advance status hierarchies. He also developed the concept of invidious distinctions to describe status hierarchies based on factors other than merit. In "*progressive change*," according to Tool (1979) and Bush (1987), instrumentally warranted values (non-invidious) supplant ceremonially warranted values (invidious). Because progressive institutional change disrupts invidious status hierarchies that interfere with social provisioning, it involves the redistribution of power and resources. Such redistributions do not reflect a "naïve harmony of interests" (see Dugger 1989, 10). In other words, while progressive institutional change advances the public interest, it may not benefit everyone.

Using this theoretical framework, neoliberalism can be viewed as a value structure that is undermining sustainable human development by elevating the level of risk experienced in daily economic life. A structural shift from a regulated form of capitalism to a resurgence of laissez-faire—neoliberalism—occurred starting in the 1970s. Neoliberalism is grounded in and espouses the view that markets are natural, rather than human constructions subject to political governance. The outcomes of market processes are depicted as efficient. The institutional hallmarks of neoliberalism are (1) globalization and market liberalization, (2) deregulation and cutbacks in social provisioning through government, (3) financialization of the economy that emphasizes the rights of shareholders, and (4) restructuring of labor markets in ways that increase instability. Neoliberal economic restructuring has heightened inequality. These unequal rewards are not based on the instrumental value of productive contributions, but rather due to the extraction of economic rents and unequal bargaining power (Folbre 2016). In particular, financialization has meant an increase in shareholder value over an emphasis on productive investments, or "workmanship" in Veblen's language (O'Hara 2006). The stories in this volume describe specific economic institutions within neoliberalism that have created problems for social provisioning, either for specific groups or for society as a whole—and the ways that these institutions are being recreated through human agency.

In sum, we human beings are products of our culture and environment. Yet we are also producers and shapers of the world in which we live. We are socialized with norms and habits but we have the capacity for consciousness that enables us to envision alternative realities. How we move from visions to new institutionalized constructs is the focus of the stories in this book.

The research method is storytelling. Storytelling can be a purposefully selected economic method (see Strassmann and Polanyi 1995). It is a bit of a lost art, unfortunately, within the economics discipline. Yet it is one that has a long history among institutional economists, who have often sought to build insights inductively from concrete experiences and case studies. Consider, for example, the insightful work of the institutionalist labor and industrial relations scholars such as Commons and, later Lloyd Reynolds (1951) and John Dunlop (1958).[2] Further, storytelling or narrative is integral to analyzing (and participating in) social movements (Olsen 2014).

In a pioneering article, Charles Wilber and Robert Harrison (1978) describe the methodology used by such institutional economists as holistic pattern modeling. Contrary to mathematical models and econometric analysis, "pattern modeling involves detailed empirical work resulting in descriptive case studies or logically consistent 'stories'" (Radzicki 1988, 634). My storytelling utilizes obtainable public information from a variety of scholarly and popular sources to delve inside institutions to examine the actions of people, groups, agents, and any rules and values (ceremonial or instrumental), with the end result being progressive institutional change. The stories in this book focus on several types of institutions, and the ways they have been transformed by social movements.

To be more specific, the eight short stories of progressive institutional change depict the importance of human agency in responding to institutional rigidities, overcoming invidious distinctions, and transforming values, habits, and customs. First, I examine changes in norms and customs regarding what does or does not "count" in measuring macroeconomic performance. This chapter interrogates GDP as the standard indicator of economic well-being and the development of satellite accounts through time use surveys that enable more comprehensive measures of how people provision. I explore the careful, steadfast work by insiders and outsiders: bureaucrats, scholars, governmental organizations, and politicians and activists. Their work represents a real moment of institutional change that lessens the invidious distinction between paid work in the labor market and unpaid work in the home.

The next story focuses on the public banking movement in the USA, a grassroots effort that offers an innovative strategy for reversing the dearth of funds for public infrastructure projects and local economic development. Though the Bank of North Dakota is the sole public bank in the USA, several states, including Vermont, are considering this model. Vermont is using a pre-existing economic development authority to help fund new housing units, green energy investments, and child care.

The succeeding three chapters explore social movements and the transformation of social practices to improve wages and working conditions for some of the lowest paid workers in the USA: retail employees (Chap. 4), migrant tomato pickers (Chap. 5), and restaurant workers (Chap. 6). In one story, activities and demonstrations of the labor-worker–community coalition called the Retail Action Project have led such major retailers as Starbucks, The Gap, Macys, and Zara to reverse their use of "on-call" shifts and to post work schedules with more advance notice. In another story, farm workers and their allies respond to new economic structures and power relations by developing innovative strategies to double their wages. The story starts in Immokalee, Florida, the fresh tomato capital of the USA. In a new model of worker organizing, the Coalition of Immokalee Workers (CIW) realized growers were themselves squeezed by large fast food companies and supermarkets in the supply chain. So the CIW went directly to food giants through their "penny a pound" movement and convinced companies to sign a Fair Food Agreement with a human rights code of conduct and independent monitoring. Today, coast to coast, at many fast food restaurants in the USA, you are eating a fair food tomato. And tomato pickers are earning more per week. Restaurant workers have also taken it upon themselves to fight for fair wages. As described in Chap. 6, a cooperative enterprise, Colors Restaurant & Bar, serves to illustrate that businesses can operate with multiple motivations beyond profit maximization. Colors is an unanticipated byproduct of Restaurant Opportunities Centers-United (ROC-U), a membership organization initially formed by restaurant workers displaced from jobs in the World Trade Center after 9/11. ROC-U operates Colors as part-restaurant, part-training facility, and part-exemplar of "high road" employment practices. ROC-U's other campaigns (such as "One Fair Wage") and litigation have secured pledges for better wages and working conditions from some larger restaurant conglomerates in the United States.

Students are fighting back, too, so they do not begin their professional careers as members of the working poor. In 2010, student loan debt surpassed credit card debt for the first time in US history. Default rates have increased following the Great Recession. Yet student debt, unlike most debt, is not dischargeable in bankruptcy, leaving those burdened by loans unable to move on with their lives. Hundreds of alumni from the private, for-profit Corinthian Colleges Inc. have proclaimed a debt strike, refusing to pay off their student loans. They assert they were defrauded by aggressive recruitment and specious promises about jobs, while Corinthian profited from federal loan funds. The seeds of this debt resistance movement, sown in the wake of Occupy Wall Street, are growing. The activism described in Chap. 7 raises questions about the provisioning and financing of higher education in the neoliberal era.

Next, I consider the amazing shift in laws and regulations brought about by the movement to advance marriage equality in the United States. In the movement for marriage equality, a combination of legal strategies and political organizing led to a change in the value structure of an institution: civil marriage. The story in Chap. 8 spotlights four key moments in legal history culminating with the *Obergefell v. Hodges* Supreme Court decision on June 26, 2015, legalizing marriage equality nationwide. These legal strategies worked in tandem with state legislation as well as other forms of activism. The analysis shows that courts do not operate in a vacuum. They are both influenced by and influence society and its changing values, with iterative feedback effects. We see that the path to marriage equality in the USA progressed—like previous civil rights moments—over decades, sometimes in waves but at other times with backlash. The redefinition of the institution of marriage can be viewed as a rejection of invidious distinctions between the romantic unions of straight couples and gay couples.

Stories of Progressive Institutional Change concludes with an analysis of consumption and production of one of the most important global commodities—coffee—and its implications for environmental sustainability. About 1.6 billion cups of coffee are consumed every day around the world. Measured by trade volume, coffee is the most important agricultural crop. It is the second most traded commodity after oil. It was also the first product to be fair trade certified and is today the leading global fair trade product. Shade-grown coffee, in particular, provides an alternative to coffee grown using agricultural practices that erode soil, over-utilize water, and decimate forest habitats. The shade-grown Rainforest Alliance and Smithsonian Migratory Bird Center bird-friendly coffees are featured. These certifications result from alliances between producers in the developing world and consumers in the United States and Europe. As described in this chapter, such certifications, though sometimes compromised, move us toward global sustainable agriculture and development practices.

Each chapter's story includes a section at the end titled "Supplementary Applications." It is intended for optional use by professors and students in the classroom. Readers, for example, are directed to data sources to discern trends, to podcasts or videos, or to websites for further examination of the issues covered in the chapter. The section contains questions for exploration and class discussion.

As the short stories demonstrate, there are multiple avenues for forging institutional change: policies, laws, cultural norms, social movements, and social practices. In challenging the neoliberal economy, groups are transforming government statistical practice, financial institutions, corporations and their treatment of workers and students, the supply chain for tomatoes, the global market for coffee beans, and civil marriage. Each of these examples involves changing values, especially reducing invidious distinctions based on artificial status. Some scholars posit that enlightened self-interest will cause individual economic actors to reach agreement upon instrumental values that support the "common interests of humanity" (see, for example, Hielscher et al. 2012, 781). The stories told in this book, though, emphasize the necessity of collective action to unseat vested interests. Supplanting ceremonial values with instrumental values is not necessarily a harmonious process and not one that occurs instantly.

Consequently, the stories are evolving. There is a long way to go, for example, before care work will be fully recognized in national statistics and remunerated fairly. Challenges to the gig economy are ongoing. Farm products like fresh tomatoes are just the tip of the iceberg, as activists focus their attention on other agricultural products. The public banking movement is gaining support across US states. Student loan activists have made an impact on raising consciousness about the burdens of debt and are beginning to influence public policy. In the USA, gay people who get legally married on a Saturday can still be fired from their jobs for who they are on a Monday. The LGBTQ civil rights movement is engaged in fighting other aspects of discrimination. Fair trade products are increasing their market share while campaigners work to improve fair trade standards worldwide.

Institutional economists are particularly adept at uncovering and analyzing social movements—the small or individual picture—in order to weave themes together and understand the bigger one. Institutional change is all around us, and there are other stories to tell. I encourage others to explore them.

Finally, I would like to acknowledge friends and colleagues who helped along the way by sharing insights, suggesting resources, and reading draft chapters: Dell Champlin, Lynne Chester, Patrick Hossay, Elaine Ingulli, Jon Luoma, Anne Mayhew, Mariam Majd, Ellen Mutari, Janice Peterson, and Linda Wharton. Ellen Mutari, you are the wind beneath my intellectual wings. My experience with Palgrave Macmillan (former Commissioning Editor Sarah Lawrence and current Editorial Assistant Allison Neuburger) has been fantastic. I am proud to be associated with the forward-looking and enterprising Palgrave Pivot series.

Notes

1. For a sociological perspective on social change within institutions, see Agustín (2015).
2. An excellent theoretical analysis of the work of John R. Commons is provided by Kaufman (2006).

References

Alesina, Alberto, and Paola Giuliano. 2015. Culture and Institutions. *Journal of Economic Literature* 53 (4): 898–944.

Agustín, Óscar García. 2015. *Sociology of Discourse: From Institutions to Social Change*. Amsterdam: John Benjamins Publishing Company.

Association for Evolutionary Economics (AFEE). 2017. Welcome. http://afee.net/. Accessed 18 Feb 2017.

Bromley, Daniel W. 2016. The 2016 Veblen-Commons Award Recipient: Daniel W. Bromley: Institutional Economics. *Journal of Economic Issues* 50 (2): 309–325.

Bush, Paul D. 1987. The Theory of Institutional Change. *Journal of Economic Issues* 21 (3): 1075–1116.

Caballero, Gonzalo, and David Soto-Oñate. 2015. The Diversity and Rapprochement of Theories of Institutional Change: Original Institutionalism and New Institutional Economics. *Journal of Economic Issues* 49 (4): 947–977.

Commons, John R. 1931. Institutional Economics. *American Economic Review* 21 (4): 648–657.

Dolfsma, Wilfred, and Rudi Verburg. 2008. Structure, Agency and the Role of Values in Processes of Institutional Change. *Journal of Economic Issues* 42 (4): 1031–1054.

Dugger, William M. 1989. Radical Institutionalism: Basic Concepts. In *Radical Institutionalism: Contemporary Voices*, ed. William M. Dugger, 1–20. Westport, CT: Greenwood Press.

Dugger, William M. 1996. Redefining Economics: From Market Allocation to Social Provisioning. In *Political Economy for the 21st Century: Contemporary Views on the Trend of Economics*, ed. Charles J. Whalen, 31–43. Armonk, NY: ME Sharpe.

Dunlop, John T. 1958. *Industrial Relations Systems*. New York: Henry Holt & Company.

Folbre, Nancy. 2016. Just Desserts? Earnings Inequality and Bargaining Power in the U.S. Economy. Working Paper 2016-10, Washington Center for Equitable Growth, Washington, DC.

Hielscher, Stefan, Ingo Pies, and Vladislav Valentinov. 2012. How to Foster Social Progress: An Ordonomic Perspective on Progressive Institutional Change. *Journal of Economic Issues* 46 (3): 779–798.

Hodgson, Geoffrey M. 2006. What Are Institutions? *Journal of Economic Issues* 40 (1): 1–25.

Kaufman, Bruce E. 2006. The Institutional Theory of John R. Commons: Foundation for a Heterodox Labor Economics. Working Paper 06-02, Andrew Young School of Policy Studies, Georgia State University, Atlanta, GA.

Mahoney, James, and Kathleen Thelen (eds.). 2009. *Explaining Institutional Change: Ambiguity, Agency, and Power*. Cambridge: Cambridge University Press.

Mayhew, Anne. 2009. Institutions. In *Handbook of Economics and Ethics*, ed. Jan Peil and Irene van Staveren, 276–282. Cheltenham: Edward Elgar.

North, Douglass. 2005. *Understanding the Process of Economic Change*. Princeton, NJ: Princeton University Press.

O'Hara, Phillip Anthony. 2006. A New Neoliberal Social Structure of Accumulation for Sustainable Global Growth and Development? In *Alternative Theories of the State*, ed. Steven Pressman, 91–112. Houndmills: Palgrave Macmillan.

Olsen, Kristine A. 2014. Telling Our Stories: Narrative and Framing in the Movement for Same-Sex Marriage. *Social Movement Studies* 13 (2): 248–266.

Radzicki, Michael J. 1988. Institutional Dynamics: An Extension of the Institutionalist Approach to Socioeconomic Analysis. *Journal of Economic Issues* 22 (3): 633–665.

Reynolds, Lloyd G. 1951. *The Structure of Labor Markets*. New York: Harper & Brothers.

Strassmann, Diana, and Livia Polanyi. 1995. The Economist as Storyteller. In *Out of the Margin: Feminist Perspectives on Economics*, ed. Edith Kuiper and Jolande Sap, 129–150. London: Routledge.

Tool, Marc R. 1979. *The Discretionary Economy: A Normative Theory of Political Economy*. Santa Monica, CA: Goodyear Publishing Company.

Tool, Marc R., and Paul Dale Bush (eds.). 2003. Preface. In *Institutional Analysis and Economic Policy*, ed. Marc R. Tool and Paul Dale Bush, xiii–xv. Boston: Kluwer Academic Publishers.

Waller, William. 2006. The Pragmatic State: Institutionalist Perspectives on the State. In *Alternatives Theories of the State*, ed. Steven Pressman, 13–33. Houndmills: Palgrave Macmillan.

Waller, William. 2017. Public Policy Adrift: Veblen's Blind Drift and Neoliberalism. *Forum for Social Economics* 46 (2): 1–11.

Wilber, Charles K., and Robert S. Harrison. 1978. The Methodological Basis of Institutional Economics: Pattern Model, Storytelling, and Holism. *Journal of Economic Issues* 12 (1): 61–89.

CHAPTER 2

Accounting for Household Production: Toward an Improved Measure of Macroeconomic Well-Being

Abstract What we measure tells us what we value. GDP is expressed in money, so only things exchanged for a price are counted in this crucial indicator of economic well-being. Housework, raising children, and other unpaid work contribute to the long-term viability of human life. But they have no price. This chapter summarizes the decade-long effort that led to the adoption of the American Time-Use Survey (ATUS) as a step toward correcting this omission in national accounts. The road involved steadfast work by insiders and outsiders: bureaucrats, scholars, governmental organizations, and politicians and activists. Their work enables more comprehensive measures of how people provision, representing a real moment of institutional change that lessens the invidious distinction between paid work in the labor market and unpaid work in the home.

Keywords Time use · Unpaid work or care work · Gross Domestic Product · Well-being · Economic indicators

JEL Codes D13 · E01 · J22 · I31

Every introductory economics student is quizzed on the definition of gross domestic product (GDP). The pat reply is "GDP is the sum of the monetary value of all goods and services produced within

© The Author(s) 2017
D.M. Figart, *Stories of Progressive Institutional Change*,
DOI 10.1007/978-3-319-59779-9_2

a nation's borders in a given year." From this definition, we learn that GDP is expressed in money, so only things exchanged for money count. Housework does not count. Neither does volunteer work. Nor work in the underground economy.[1]

Hopefully, students are also introduced to critiques about the limits of GDP as a measure of economic well-being. It is crucial to recognize that the US National Income and Product Accounts (NIPA) from which GDP is derived are based on conventions—that is, institutionalized norms about which data are or are not collected and counted. These conventions not only reflect particular social values but also reinforce them in a process of cumulative causation. This causes a rigidity in this institution. Specifically, the way we measure GDP reflects a view that conflates the economy with markets. "The economy" equals the market system. Other institutions involved in social provisioning are rendered secondary or external to what is being measured. NIPA is thus an institutionalized expression of the primacy of markets and the silencing of other forms of social provisioning.

My first short story of institutional change summarizes efforts to change this convention and find a way to count non-market activities that contribute to social provisioning. Time use studies produced by the US Bureau of Labor Statistics (BLS) are slowly being incorporated into non-market satellite accounts at the Bureau of Economic Analysis (BEA) of the US Department of Commerce—the people who bring us GDP. A decade-long effort inside and outside the US government ultimately led to the adoption of the American Time-Use Survey (ATUS). The federal budget for ATUS was first proposed in 2000 in President Bill Clinton's budget request and approved by the US Congress. ATUS is now an ongoing official statistical program of the US government, prominently lessening the invidious distinction between paid work in the labor market and unpaid work in the home (Figart 2003). The road to how we got there involves careful, steadfast work by insiders and outsiders alike: hard-working bureaucrats, scholars, governmental organizations, and politicians and activists.

FEMINISTS ARGUE FOR TIME USE STUDIES

The seeds of the first federally funded and continuous ATUS in 2003 were sown decades earlier, at the same time that Simon Kuznets was doing extensive work on national income and products accounts. In the 1930s, Margaret Reid wrote the *Economics of Household Production* (1934), based on her dissertation at the University of Chicago under her Ph.D. advisor, Hazel Kyrk. As summarized by Nancy Folbre, "In the first half of the twentieth century, interest in counting non-market work occasionally cropped up only to wilt beneath the disapproving eye of the economic orthodoxy" (2009, 260). In the introduction to a special issue of *Feminist Economics* on the life of work of Margaret Reid, Folbre relates, "Occasional efforts to calculate the contribution of 'homemakers' were met with disinterest and derision until women comprised a significant share of the economics profession" (1996, xii).

In empirical research, home economists following Margaret Reid pursued the study of time allocation as a means to computing monetary equivalents for housework, coincident with the second wave of feminism in the USA. For example, *Time Use* was an extensive, detailed major study by Kathryn E. Walker and Margaret E. Woods (1976), published by the American Home Economics Association, in which authors assessed food preparation, care of family members, care of the house, care of clothing, and managing the house. Among other outcomes, Walker and Woods found that women who worked as full-time homemakers averaged 57 h of work per week (8.1 h per day) at home, a full-time job (1976, Table 3.14). Furthermore, men's hours of work in the home did not increase in concert with women's increase in hours in the paid labor market, leading to later scholarship on what is termed a "second shift." About 70% of the work in the home was done by wives, with husbands and children providing about 15% each on average.

Feminist political economists have long argued that the National Income and Product Accounts (NIPA) did not recognize or value work in the home, including child care. Theoretically, in the 1980s, early feminist economists such as Lourdes Benería, Heidi Hartmann, and Susan Himmelweit borrowed the term "social reproduction" from Marxism and used it as an analytical category. Hartmann (1981, 373) argues that "[t]he system of production in which we live cannot be understood without reference to the production and re-production both of commodities—whether in factories, service centers, or offices—and of people, in households." Some feminists in Britain fashioned a "wages for housework" campaign to value the work of home production.

In the US, a number of time-use studies followed (for a summary, see Hartmann 1981, 377–386; for earlier studies, see Walker and Woods 1976, 4–5), further substantiating Walker and Woods's *Time Use*. Much of the evidence was gathered through 24-h time diaries, considered a highly reliable method. The Universities of Michigan and Maryland, for example, have conducted such time-use surveys periodically since 1965. A few studies were supplemented by extensive interviews/field visits with a subset of the sample (see Power 1977), with the latter approach proving to be too expensive for widespread adoption by ATUS. Collection and analysis of time use data were done in other countries as well, but not yet as part of a national statistical, consistent, and reliable longitudinal survey.

In the late 1980s, a feminist politician in New Zealand took up the mantle, devoting much of her career to ensuring that national income accounting would be rid of gender discrimination. She is Marilyn Waring, a sociologist by training and a former member of the New Zealand parliament. As head of the Public Expenditure Committee, Waring became familiar with the intricate details of the United Nations (UN) system of national accounts. Her (1988) book, *If Women Counted*, became an important manifesto in feminist economics and was made into a 1995 documentary film titled *Who's Counting? Marilyn Waring on Sex, Lies and Global Economics*. In the book, Waring penned a sophisticated critique of the omission of unpaid work in the household, though she also discussed that no value was given for volunteer services, either. In fact, she went as far as describing the UN system of national accounts as "applied patriarchy" (Saunders and Dalziel 2017, 201). (Today, the imputed value of volunteer labor is often reported by organizations in their annual accounting statements and summaries of such value nationally.) Waring's research sparked discussion and political organizing throughout the globe around the work of counting household labor.[2]

This included the United Nations World Conference to Review and Appraise the Achievements of the United Nations Decade for Women conference in Nairobi, Kenya, in 1985. The recommendations arising from this key conference of politicians, scholars, non-governmental organizations (NGOs) and activists include a commitment to measuring and valuing unpaid work with timely and reliable statistics, albeit a limited one: "Governments should compile gender-specific statistics and information and should develop or reorganize an information system to take decisions and action on the advancement of women" (paragraph 130), e.g., statistics that "reflect accurately women's contribution to food staples" (paragraph 179) and caregiving (United Nations 1986).

The governments of Australia, Finland, Denmark, Germany, Sweden, Norway, and Canada were among the first industrialized countries to employ time-use surveys. In 1981, Statistics Canada piloted a national time-use study to help value non-market activities, with the time-use survey becoming fully implemented in 1986, 2 years before Marilyn Waring's influential book. Australian economist Duncan Ironmonger played a central role in development and promoting time use in that country.[3] A pilot time use survey under the Australian Bureau of Statistics (ABS) was conducted as early as 1987. The 1990s saw sweeping advancements in the global effort to measure and value unpaid work. Statistics Canada sponsored an international conference on the topic of unpaid work in 1993. The US BLS sent representatives. After a multi-year process, that same year, the United Nations international standard system of national accounts (SNA)—first employed in 1953—published a second revision that names household activities as "productive in an economic sense" (SNA 1993, 5). In effect, this meant valuing household goods production for their own consumption in the measurement, but excluding cooking, cleaning, child care, and elder care. This was the first step, as the SNA cannot be enforced in national governments.

Globally, with a dozen countries as models completing one or more time-use surveys, delegates to the 1995 United Nations Fourth Conference on Women in Beijing, China, were teeming with renewed interest in national action to measure and consider household production in making public policy. The resultant Platform for Action included a number of endorsements for gender-sensitive policies and programs. Paragraph 206 is perhaps the most significant in a call for a strategic objective to generate and disseminate gender-disaggregated data for planning and evaluation, for instance:

> Developing methods, in the appropriate forums, for assessing the value, in quantitative terms, of unremunerated work that is outside national accounts, such as caring for dependents and preparing food, for possible reflection in satellite or other official accounts that may be produced separately from but are consistent with core national accounts, with a view to recognizing the economic contribution of women and making visible the unequal distribution of remunerated and unremunerated work between women and men. (United Nations 1996, Paragraph 206(f)(iii))

In 1996, the Canadian census queried citizens for the first time about time spent on unpaid housework. The USA still lagged behind at that point.

The Road to the American Time Use Survey[4]

Between 1995 and 1997, a BLS working group contracted with a survey firm to pilot test two alternative time-use questionnaires using telephone interviews, the method ultimately chosen for data collection to substantiate information in time diaries. A study based on the data was conducted in 1997. Getting respected economists and specialists in the USA to embrace the idea, moving it from the margin to the center, was vital to the success of ATUS. (Thorstein Veblen would likely have embraced this role for technical expertise.)

The BLS reached out to the MacArthur Foundation's Research Network on Family and the Economy (1997–2003) to cosponsor a two-day conference on "Time Use, Non-market Work, and Family Well-Being". Nancy Folbre, an expert on social reproduction and caring labor and a member of the network, presented a paper (Folbre 1997). So did economist Duncan Ironmonger from Australia, but who presented on the European Union's (EU) plans for a harmonized method for cross-country time-use surveys. In a sense, the conference experts served as cheerleaders for the BLS time-use pilot. Attendees wanted the work to continue in a significant way. Although not unanimous, two crucial endorsements emerged: (1) Individual paper time diaries are the best method of data collection, as used in Australia, as long as respondents were able to record primary and secondary activities (what else were you doing while minding a child or doing the dishes?) and (2) Computer-Aided Telephone Interviews (CATI) would corroborate diary findings and probe about secondary activities.

Members of the National Academy of Sciences (NAS/NRC) who attended the conference wanted to hold a similar workshop in 1998. This time, in addition to inviting academics and representatives of the BLS and other federal agencies, the NAS sought to involve the Committee on National Statistics (CNSTAT), another group of top experts. Important here is that the inclusion of CNSTAT brought notable economists and statisticians like William Nordhaus from Yale and Joseph G. Altonji and Charles F. Manski from Northwestern to the table with longtime time-use researchers and advocates like Nancy Folbre (University of Massachusetts-Amherst), Michael Bittman (University of New South Wales, Australia), John P. Robinson and Suzanne Bianchi (University of Maryland), F. Thomas Juster (University of Michigan), and Daniel Hamermesh (University of Texas-Austin). To say the least, a significant achievement was marked by CNSTAT's validation of the BLS's work and approach to data collection. A report of the workshop, published in 2000 claims that "[d]ata on time use are important sources of information, and the lack of national time-use data is a critical gap in the federal statistical system" (NRC 2000, 58).

In my view, the imprimatur of the 15-member 1999–2000 Committee on National Statistics, only one of whom was gendered female (demographer Julie DaVanzo from RAND who served as Workshop Chair), meant that the US government could not turn away from instituting a time-use survey. The subsequent funding of ATUS in the federal budget in 2000 led to field testing, hiring of interviewers, staff training, and publication, as well as data dissemination planning. The full launch in January of 2003 was—and remains—a collaboration between the BLS and the US Census Bureau, as the representative sample of households is drawn from the Bureau's monthly Current Population Survey.

To take the next step in discussing how to employ time-use data to design non-market accounts for the NIPA, the National Academy of Sciences assembled the eleven-person expert "Panel to Study the Design of Nonmarket Accounts." Nancy Folbre was a member of this panel, and so were Katharine Abraham—former BLS Commissioner under whom ATUS was piloted—and Barbara Fraumeni of the US Department of Commerce (later taking a position at the University of Southern Maine). Among the recommendations of the Panel were:

> Recommendation 2.1: The American Time Use Survey, which can be used to quantify time inputs into productive nonmarket activity, should underpin the construction of supplemental national accounts for the United States. To serve effectively in this role, the survey should be ongoing and conducted in a methodologically consistent manner over time. (Abraham and Mackie 2005, 7)

Early Evidence of the Significance of Time Use Research

Although ATUS is a young statistical survey, its value has been proven through the rich scholarship that has been forthcoming from data analysis. We have a better understanding of how people allocate their time (see, e.g., Kimmel 2008). These time allocation data are critical to gauging the value of the home production sector and measuring its productivity. We have not changed the definition of GDP yet and it still remains the dominant measure of macroeconomic performance. Nevertheless, we now have estimates that would adjust GDP for household production. For example, the level of GDP would have risen by 39% in 1965, 27% in 2004, and 26% in 2010. The adjusted percent increase is higher in 1965 because of the relatively greater hours that women spent in home production in 1965 as compared to 2010 (Landefeld et al. 2009; Bridgman et al. 2012). Another estimate of the value of child care alone exceeds these previous estimates for 2004 and 2010, for an upward adjustment to GDP of 43% (Suh and Folbre 2016). The development of satellite accounts within the BEA thus represents a real moment of institutional change.

Compared to other developed countries, the USA has been relatively "late to the party" in employing time use research to development household satellite accounts. Norway, though, was an early pioneer. During the 1970s, the valued added in household production in Norwegian GDP was roughly 40% of GDP. As women increased their hours in the paid labor market, the value added has declined and measured 24% of GDP in 2000 (Aslaksen and Koren 2014). Household production in Finland added 39% to GDP in 2006 (Varjonen and Kirjavainen 2014). The imputed value of unpaid household work, and volunteer and community work in Australia, was estimated at 43.5% in 2006, placing it near the highest among international comparisons along with New Zealand, Japan, and Portugal. Among the lowest estimates are the countries of Canada, Korea, China, and the USA (ABS 2014, Graph 1). It important to note that country rankings can shift based on which valuation method is used for household production.

Women across the world, it is said, experience time poverty. While technology may be able to help complete domestic tasks easier and more quickly, there are only a fixed number of hours in a day. It is well documented that women perform more housework and caregiving than men.

This leaves women relatively less time for sleep, leisure, and exercise, to name a few. In terms of public policy, we first need to measure time use. Work conducted within households is an important economic activity. We need a harmonized method of time use as well as valuation in GDP for better cross-country comparisons. This chapter profiled the development of the American Time Use Survey as a great leap forward. Last, but certainly not least, we need improvements in public policy to help better balance paid work and family time. It is not just paid family leave. Or the availability of affordable and high-quality child and elder care. Instead, accounting for housework, the title of this chapter, also means questioning the traditional hegemonic model of long paid working hours that assume that there is someone at home full time or part time taking care of the necessary and undervalued activities to sustain well-being. Current policy discussions in the USA include proposals to expand and modernize Social Security benefits, recognizing the lifetime benefit loss for caregivers and widows and widowers. If adopted, such an expansion would provide another tangible recognition of household production.

Notes

1. A history of the GDP measure, the roles it plays in policymaking, and its importance is found in Diane Coyle's book, *GDP: A Brief but Affectionate History* (2014). Coyle is less critical than feminists, though, about GDP as a measure of economic welfare (Coyle 2014).
2. *Counting on Marilyn Waring* is an excellent volume devoted to the influence of Waring's work (Bjørnholt and McKay 2014).
3. Among Ironmonger's prolific work, I would recommend his article in *Feminist Economics* (1996).
4. My summary of the development of ATUS inside the US government draws extensively upon an article that was coauthored by Michael Horrigan of the US Bureau of Labor Statistics (BLS), who served as the survey's director (Horrigan and Herz 2004).

Supplementary Applications

1. Write down three unpaid tasks that you spent time on in the last week. Calculate how many hours you spent on the task. Compare the amount of time you spent with the latest averages from the American Time Use Survey (ATUS).

2. Many countries of the world now utilize time use surveys. Multicountry statistical agencies also conduct time use research, such as Eurostat, the statistical agency of the European Union, and the Organisation for Economic Co-operation and Development (family data and the OECD Better Life Index). Explore official government websites for time use surveys. Look at differences in households tasks, child care, leisure, and paid labor by gender in two different countries and summarize your findings. See, for example, that Norwegian men are most helpful with housework while Japanese men do the least.
3. Find countries that have used time use surveys to impute a value for the contribution of unpaid productive labor in satellite accounts (for estimates of additions to GDP). For one of these countries, discuss the impact of household labor on the country's GDP. The United Nations Statistics Division provides an introductory overview of time-use research across the globe, with some links to time use investigations in over 70 countries.
4. Investigate other measures of economic well-being besides GDP. How, for example, is the Genuine Progress Indicator (GPI) different than GDP?
5. Melinda Gates (of the Bill and Melinda Gates Foundation) gave an interview on women's time poverty with "Marketplace," the National Public Radio show, on March 21, 2016. In the exchange with host David Brancaccio, Gates intermixes data (from the USA, Europe, and Africa) with personal reflections based on time spent living in Tanzania. Gates also discusses policy needs, especially for working adults in the US. Write a reaction to what she argues and suggest other policy remedies that may help households reduce their so-called time poverty.

References

Abraham, Katherine G., and Christopher Mackie (eds.). 2005. *Beyond the Market: Designing Nonmarket Accounts for the United States*. Washington, DC: National Academy of Sciences.

Aslaksen, Iulie and Charlotte Koren. 2014. Reflections on Unpaid Household Work, Economic Growth, and Consumption Possibilities. In *Counting on*

Marilyn Waring, ed. Margunn Bjørnholt and Ailsa McKay, 55–69. Bradford, ON: Demeter Press.

Australian Bureau of Statistics (ABS). 2014. Spotlight on the National Accounts: Unpaid Work in the Australian Economy. May 2014. http://www.abs.gov.au/AusStats/ABS@.nsf/Latestproducts/5202.0Main%20Features1May%202014?opendocument&tabname=Summary&prodno=5202.0&issue=May%202014&num=&view=.

Bjørnholt, Margunn, and Ailsa McKay (eds.). 2014. *Counting on Marilyn Waring: New Advances in Feminist Economics*, 2nd ed. Bradford, ON: Demeter Press.

Bridgman, Benjamin, Andrew Dugan, Mikhael Lal, Matthew Osborne, and Shaunda Villones. 2012. Accounting for Household Production in the National Accounts, 1965–2010. *Survey of Current Business* 92 (5): 23–36.

Coyle, Diane. 2014. *GDP: A Brief but Affectionate History*. Princeton, NJ: Princeton University Press.

Figart, Deborah M. 2003. Policies to Provide Non-Invidious Employment. In *Institutional Analysis and Economic Policy*, ed. Marc R. Tool and Paul D. Bush, 379–409. Dordrecht: Kluwer Academic.

Folbre, Nancy. 1996. Introduction: For Margaret, With Thanks. *Feminist Economics* 2 (3): xi–xii.

Folbre, Nancy. 1997. A Time (Use Survey) for Every Purpose: Non-Market Work and the Production of Human Capabilities. Paper presented at the Conference on Time Use, Non-market Work, and Family Well-Being, November 20–21, Washington, DC.

Folbre, Nancy. 2009. *Greed, Lust & Gender: A History of Economic Ideas*. Oxford: Oxford University Press.

Hartmann, Heidi I. 1981. The Family as a Locus of Gender, Class, and Political Struggle: The Example of Housework. *Signs: Journal of Women in Culture and Society* 6 (3): 366–394.

Horrigan, Michael and Diane Herz. 2004. Planning, Designing, and Executing the BLS American Time-Use Survey. *Monthly Labor Review* October: 3–19.

Ironmonger, Duncan. 1996. Counting Outputs, Capital Input and Caring Labor: Estimating Gross Household Product. *Feminist Economics* 2 (3): 37–64.

Kimmel, Jean, (ed.). 2008. *How Do We Spend Our Time? Evidence from the American Time Use Survey*. Kalamazoo, MI: W.E. Upjohn Institute for Employment Research.

Landefeld, J. Steven, Barbara M. Fraumeni, and Cindy M. Vojtech. 2009. Accounting for Household Production: A Prototype Satellite Account using the American Time Use Survey. *Review of Income and Wealth* 55 (2): 205–225.

National Research Council (NRC). 2000. *Time-Use Measurement and Research: Report of a Workshop*, ed. Michele Ver Ploeg, Joseph Altonji, Norman Bradburn, Julie DaVanzo, William Nordhaus, and Francisco Samaniego. Washington, DC: National Academies Press.

Power Marilyn. 1977. Housework as a Production Activity: Changes in the Content and Organization of Housework. Ph.D dissertation, University of California-Berkeley, Berkeley.

Reid, Margaret. 1934. *Economics of Household Production*. New York: Wiley.

Saunders, Caroline, and Paul Dalziel. 2017. Twenty-Five Years of Counting for Nothing: Waring's Critique of National Accounts. *Feminist Economics* 23 (2): 200–218.

Suh, Jooyeoun, and Nancy Folbre. 2016. Valuing Unpaid Child Care in the US: A Prototype Satellite Account Using the American Time Use Survey. *Review of Income and Wealth* 62 (4): 668–684.

System of National Accounts. 1993. http://unstats.un.org/unsd/nationalaccount/docs/1993sna.pdf.

United Nations. 1986. *Report of the World Conference to Review and Appraise the Achievements of the United Nations Decade for Women: Equality, Development and Peace*. New York: UN.

United Nations. 1996. *Report of the Fourth World Conference on Women, Beijing, September 4–15, 1995*. New York: UN.

Varjonen, Johanna and Leena M. Kirjavainen. 2014. Women's Unpaid Work was Counted but …. In *Counting on Marilyn Waring*, ed. Margunn Bjørnholt and Ailsa McKay, 71–87. Bradford,ON: Demeter Press.

Walker, Kathryn E., and Margaret E. Woods. 1976. *The Time Use: A Measure of Household Production of Family Goods and Services*. Washington, DC: American Home Economics Association.

Waring, Marilyn. 1988. *If Women Counted: A New Feminist Economics*. San Francisco: HarperCollins.

CHAPTER 3

Funding Infrastructure and Local Economic Development: A Public Bank Option

Abstract D+ is not a Grade Point Average to be proud of. Yet that is the current assessment of America's infrastructure by the American Society of Civil Engineers. One grassroots effort offers an innovative strategy for reversing the dearth of funds for infrastructure projects and local economic development: the public banking movement. The Bank of North Dakota, the sole public bank in the USA established in 1919, serves as a model for the newly revived movement. No state has progressed further than Vermont. In 2014, Vermont took a stride toward a state-owned bank by authorizing a new Local Investment Advisory Committee to help steer a public lending program through a pre-existing economic development authority. Funds are supporting new housing units, green energy investments, and the child care industry.

Keywords Public bank · Economic development · Infrastructure · Public finance · Financial inclusion

JEL Codes E5 · E44 · G21 · H41

D+ is not a Grade Point Average to be proud of. Yet sadly, that is the current assessment of America's infrastructure by the American Society of Civil Engineers (ASCE 2017). In the 2017 *Report Card of America's Infrastructure*, grades were determined for major US infrastructure categories such as drinking water (a D grade), roads (D), dams (D), energy (D+), parks and recreation (D+), schools (D+), wastewater treatment (D+), bridges (C+), and ports (C+). Report cards for most of the 50 US states individually also hover in the C-to-D range.

Even more disheartening, the USA has received a near-failing infrastructure Grade Point Average from the ASCE in every 4-year appraisal since the ASCE started these comprehensive assessments in 1998. Neglect of infrastructure is not a recent problem. The D+ average is a marginal improvement from a D in 2009. Efforts to redress some of the nation's most vulnerable bridges were aided by short-term boosts in federal funding on infrastructure to aid in recovery from the Great Recession, as well as greater investment in rail; this additional spending helped inch the infrastructure GPA higher by 2013. These temporary infusions, however, are a drop in the bucket. To remedy deficiencies, ASCE estimates that plugging the investment gap (to earn a B average) by 2025 would cost $4.59 trillion in constant dollars; not acting would reduce GDP by $3.9 trillion over the next 10 years.

Infrastructure is a major aspect of our national economic provisioning so neglecting it is unsustainable in the long run. The ASCE opened its 2013 report card by pointing out that "Every family, every community and every business needs infrastructure to thrive" (2013, 4). In his (1958) book *The Affluent Society*, John Kenneth Galbraith termed this problem a lack of *social balance.* Galbraith asserted that overreliance on private sector market mechanisms intrinsically leads to underfunding of public infrastructure—not only roads and bridges but also parks, education, public services, and mass transportation. Optimal social balance between private and public goods and services requires countervailing power embedded in democratically responsive institutions. Such institutions are more responsive than for-profit businesses to social needs.

The dearth of funds for investment in public goods and services in a tax-resistant culture can be challenged directly through political processes, by advocating infrastructure spending on the federal, state, and local levels. But this is not the only possible tack. One grassroots effort that offers an innovative strategy for funding infrastructure projects, as well as for nurturing local economic development projects, is the public banking movement. A public bank (or a state-owned bank) is a bank that is owned by a representative government. It is indirectly owned by the people of a locality and, therefore, operates under the mission of working toward the public interest. The state (or locality) deposits its revenue in its own financial institution, rather than banking with a private sector "big bank." To this point, the Bank of North Dakota, established in 1919, remains the sole public bank in the USA. It serves as a model for a newly revived movement.

The Bank of North Dakota (BND) demonstrates how public banks institutionalize countervailing power and serve the public interest. Peter Fisher (1983), analyzing the BND model, argues that public banks would promote:

1. Individual growth and development;
2. Equality and cooperation in social relationships;
3. Social and biological continuity; and
4. Expansion of knowledge and free inquiry.

Fisher refers to these four standards as social value criteria and argues that institutions that meet all four represent progressive institutional change. Based on these criteria, Fisher maintains that public banks under democratic political control represent a more thorough progressive vision than simply tightening regulations on private sector banks. They achieve this by channeling investment funds into depressed regions (thus spurring local economic development), stemming the outflow of capital from neighborhoods, pooling resources from a broader area than local banks, and allowing for democratic participation.

In the years since the Great Recession, over twenty US states have introduced bills for state-owned banks and/or to study their feasibility. The deregulation of banking in recent decades has intensified the rationale for public banking since private sector financial institutions are far less grounded in localities than they were in a more regulated era. Big banks utilize their deposits wherever they anticipate the highest return. Further, the recession itself was triggered by the collapse of a housing bubble generated, at least in part, by a misallocation of resources by private banking interests. Public banks, in contrast, invest government funds locally in projects that support economic development efforts and return profits to the state to replenish its coffers. Therefore, public banks offer an institutional mechanism to address the crisis in the quality of public infrastructure, as well as unfulfilled demand for credit by small businesses and farmers.

Context for the Contemporary Public Banking Movement

Public banks are in nearly every region of the world.[1] Globally, the height of state banking for development and public infrastructure came in the post-World War II and post-colonial (independence) periods. In countries where economic institutions are not sufficiently developed for private banks to meet financing needs, government has stepped into remedy market failure and stimulate growth. Estimates indicate that by the late 1970s government-owned banks controlled 40% of combined banking assets in developed countries and 65% of assets in developing countries. Subsequently, public banks fell out of favor in the neoliberal era. Privatization resulted in the share of assets in state-owned banks falling to 22% of banking assets in developing countries and 8% in advanced countries (Marois 2013, 2).

Public banking was never as popular in the United States; only one state bank, the Bank of North Dakota (BND), was established during the Progressive Era in 1919.[2] Despite numerous accounts documenting the BND's longstanding success (for example, Fettig 1994; Harkinson 2009; Brown 2013; Rapoport 2013; Schneiberg 2013), this exemplary model has only recently generated serious consideration by other states. The political economic context, however, has changed since the early twentieth century when the first public bank took root in a nascent and decentralized financial industry. Today's public banking movement has to respond to the entrenched interests of not only existing banks but also the myriad of existing state development agencies.

In *The Public Bank Solution*, Ellen Brown, the founder and President of the Public Banking Institute, argues: "A functioning economy needs credit to flow freely. What impairs this flow is that the spigots are under private control" (2013, 2). A select number of very large national private banks hold the overwhelming majority of state deposits. In the private model, shareholders may live nowhere near where banks are located and profits can go anywhere, not necessarily reinvested back in the local community. Instead, "The public model sees interest and profits from banking as belonging *to the community*, and the wealth they generate is re-invested in the community" (Brown 2014, 1, emphasis original).

The global financial crisis in 2008 contributed to skepticism about a purely market-centered paradigm for finance and renewed interest in alternatives such as state-owned banks. The contemporary case for public banks focuses on misallocation of resources by private banking institutions leading to underfunding of public infrastructure and community redevelopment; public banks also provide other direct and indirect (multiplier) impacts such as increases to state GDP, income, and employment. The public bank movement is also stirred by small farmers and business owners who claim that bank lending since the Great Recession has been deficient. In fact, based on Federal Deposit Insurance Corporation (FDIC) data of bank balance sheets, small business lending has decreased in both the absolute and relative sense (Mills and McCarthy 2014; Wiersch 2015). According to one Harvard Business School study, "A decades-long trend toward consolidation of banking assets in fewer institutions is eliminating a key source of capital for small firms" (Mills and McCarthy 2014, 6). Further, state-owned banks may be able to reduce the cost of public policy by lending at lower interest rates, and avoiding asset bubbles with more evened out debt cycles. Some portion of the revenue (surplus) may be returned to supplement state budgets to enable more spending and/or reduced tax rates.

Across the US, interest is widespread, with no geographic or demographic pattern. States pursuing measures include highly urbanized states such as Massachusetts, California, and New York, to more rural states such as Maine, Vermont, and Montana, and states diverse as Hawaii, Oregon, Colorado, and Washington State. Cities with an interest in a local, municipal bank include Santa Fe (NM); the Pennsylvania cities of Philadelphia, Pittsburgh, Allentown, and Reading; Washington State cities of Seattle and Tacoma; and San Francisco (Figart and Majd 2016). The list is growing. These efforts are supported by progressive organizations such as the Public Banking Institute (PBI) and Dēmos. In the USA, the non-profit PBI was founded in 2011 to promote research about state and locally owned banks.

Thus far, the BND public banking model has not fully migrated to other states. Advocates have run head-on into an influential banking lobby in state legislatures. Nevertheless, several states have taken tangible steps that are laying the groundwork for transitioning current economic development institutions toward the public banking model. Perhaps no state has progressed further than the state of Vermont. Vermont has taken the first measured stride toward a state-owned bank by authorizing a new Local Investment Advisory Committee to help steer a new public lending program through a pre-existing economic development authority.

The Bank of North Dakota as a Reference Point

In the early twentieth century, the North Dakota economy was dependent on farming. Statistically, US counties with elite agricultural landowners with large landholdings had fewer banks per capita. As a result, credit was costlier, and less obtainable (Ratjan and Ramcharran 2011), hampering farmers who need seed and supplies before a crop yield makes it to market. And a successful harvest is far from uncertain with the vagaries of weather. A populist movement spurred the creation of the BND to help farmers secure access to credit "at cost" or close to it. Specifically, an agrarian reform movement called the Nonpartisan League (NPL) sought to shift power from the so-called big money interests (in neighboring Minneapolis and St. Paul, Minnesota, and Chicago, Illinois) to the people. Founded in 1915 originally as a North Dakota party, the NPL advocated state control of the banks and farm-related industries such as grain mills. In 1916, the NPL won the North Dakota governorship (candidate Lynn Frazier) as well as the majority of seats in the state House of Representatives. A public Bank of North Dakota Act passed in 1919, and BND opened on June 20, 1919, capitalized with $2 million through the sale of state bonds.

Headquartered in Bismarck, North Dakota, BND currently holds over $1 billion in assets and is one of the largest banks in the state (Fettig 1994). Its primary mission was (and is) to promote state agriculture, commerce, and industry, and stimulate economic development through lending. According to former North Dakota Governor Ed Schafer (1992–2000), "A development mentality is different from a banking mentality" (quoted in Fettig 1994, 4). BND does not directly compete with private banks, and consequently the North Dakota Bankers' Association endorses BND as a complementary institution.[3] Such support by traditional bankers is lacking in other states. In short, the main features of BND, gleaned from annual reports on the website, are:

- All funds of the state and state institutions must be deposited with the bank. (Most deposits come from the state.)
- The deposits are guaranteed by the state, not the federal government (FDIC). (Even so, note that FDIC insurance is limited per account holder.)

- Consumer lending is generally restricted to farming-related loans, as opposed to auto loans and residential mortgages. Yet over the decades, BND has become a broader lender, holding a large portfolio of federally insured student loans for the benefit of students in the state.
- The bank has a bank president but its activities are governed by an Industrial Commission (the governor, attorney general, and the commissioner of agriculture).
- BND transfers about half of its surplus funds (profits) to the legislature and the usage of bank earnings is at the discretion of the legislature.

BND also partners with private local lenders for community-based loans to stimulate local economic development. One example is a loan program titled Partnership in Assisting Community Expansion (PACE). PACE loans to businesses have added thousands of jobs, though job creation is not required for all lending. Businesses and community development associations may borrow for a variety of purposes—playgrounds and day care facilities, expansion of medical facilities, investing in green technology, affordable housing, etc. (Schmitz 2016).

Unlike private banks and finance companies, BND never engaged in subprime lending. It did not face a credit crunch during the financial crisis. North Dakota continues to have one of the lowest unemployment rates in the USA and a continuous budget surplus (since 2008). BND has helped play a role in these resilient economic outcomes, and bank leadership points this out whenever asked. In one interview, current BND President and CEO Eric Hardmeyer has said: "We take those funds and then, really what separates us is that we plow those deposits back into the state of North Dakota in the form of loans. We invest back into the state in economic development type of activities. We grow our state through that mechanism." In answering a follow-up question, Hardmeyer declares BND invests a larger portion of the money into the state's economy [than a private bank would] (quoted in Harkinson 2009). The BND model, however, is not without detractors. Critics point to numerous problems and limitations with state banks. They allege that private banks have higher profits and better balance sheets. State banks are less efficient, run by bureaucrats, putting public revenues at risk. State banks, it is argued, are also not any better for state economic development than private banks. They challenge the lack of freely flowing credit in private financial markets. Further, critics contend, the success of the only US state-owned bank is due chiefly to the state's oil boom.

Individual scholars and organizations have weighed in on this debate through empirical research. Some studies have tilted against state-owned banks (e.g., various studies by the World Bank), others have shown mixed results (Yeyati et al. 2007), and still others positive (von Mettenheim 2012; Marois 2013). My intention here is not to respond to this point-counterpoint. The impact of state-owned and locally owned banks is best ascertained by estimates provided in high-quality feasibility studies; these studies indicate that while the institutional context has changed in the century since the BND was founded, private financial markets still do not fully address social needs and can be augmented by innovative new forms of public banking.

VERMONT: ONE STRIDE TOWARD A PUBLIC BANK TO SPUR ECONOMIC DEVELOPMENT

Vermont, despite its deservedly progressive reputation, suffers from the typical lack of social balance between private and public goods and services. Vermont's public infrastructure is falling apart—roads, bridges, dams, drinking water facilities, and wastewater treatment. In 2010, the USA and Vermont Departments of Transportation and the American Society of Civil Engineers gave the state poor grades on its public infrastructure. Overall, Vermont received a C− rating; bridges were C−, dams were C, drinking water was C−, roads were D+, and wastewater was D+ (*Exploring a Public Bank for Vermont* 2013, 7). And like 49 other state governments, most of the State of Vermont's deposits are in large private banks who are not serving the public interest. Assessing bank concentration using FDIC data, Jason Judd and Heather McGhee from Dēmos (2012) calculated that four of the five largest banks are chartered out-of-state and control more than 57% of all Vermont deposits (TD Bank, Peoples Bank, RBS/Citizens, and KeyBank). The largest, TD Bank, is home to more than 22% of all Vermont deposits. But, as Judd and McGhee show, TD Bank has loaned relatively little to small businesses through the Small Business Administration (SBA) loan program. Further, big bank interest rates are too high for business loans, municipal loans, and credit card interest, Judd and McGhee assert.

Vermont came close to establishing a state bank in 2014 and, in the process, its advocates developed an innovative plan for converting existing economic development agencies into a state bank. Although the ultimate result was one step shy of institutionalizing a public bank, the groundwork laid by these activists is instructive. A coalition of organizers, businesses, and individuals called Vermonters for a New Economy came together to support a movement for a new public (state) bank. A public bank, it was argued, would be better able to fulfill the state's unmet capital needs. Advocates pointed out that for decades, the State of North Dakota has been reaping the benefits of the only public bank in the USA; Vermont could, too. Their champion in the Vermont legislature was State Senator Anthony Pollina of Middlesex in Washington County, a former advisor to US Senator Bernie Sanders.

Besides introducing bills outright for a state-owned bank, Senator Pollina also introduced bills in the 2011–2012 and 2013–2014 sessions to study the impact of a state bank in Vermont. Interest was spurred by a citizen's committee for a Vermont Partnership Bank/State Bank as well as studies by the Vermont Legislative Joint Fiscal Office (2010), the then-Center for State Innovation (Judd and Munger 2010), and Dēmos (Judd and McGhee 2012). Vermonters for a New Economy and the League of Women Voters of Vermont helped raise funds for a public bank economic impact study. The Vermont Bankers' Association was critical of even studying the issue in the first place, later testifying against public lending in the Vermont legislature.

The Gund Institute of the University of Vermont and the Political Economy Research Institute at the University of Massachusetts completed the technical analysis for the state bank economic impact study. *Exploring a Public Bank for Vermont: Economic Impacts, Capital Needs, and Implementation* was released in December of 2013. Using standard input–output analysis and assuming $236.2 million in public bank lending, the Vermont report estimated the following potential benefits: 2535 new jobs; $192 million added to Gross State Product; $342 million increase in state output (due to multiplier effects); and savings of $100 million on interest costs over 20 years. These were considered lower bound estimates since many of the potential positive benefits related to student loans, municipal bonds (ratings and interest rates), and partnerships with large private banks were not factored into the analysis.

In order to remain objective and be responsive to potential criticism, *Exploring a Public Bank for Vermont* also investigated whether public bank credit would be additional lending or would it simply reduce private bank lending proportionately, due to the withdrawal of state funds from private banks. The report found no evidence to support the hypothesis that public bank lending would simply crowd out private bank lending. Rather, it would add to total lending in the state. According to the report, "A fundamental question we have tried to answer is whether or not credit created by a public bank in Vermont would be new credit that was not previously being loaned by private banks. We have provided evidence that it would be, and have done a projection of the impact of $236 million of new loans in the state of Vermont, showing the job and output metrics are significant" (*Exploring a Public Bank for Vermont* 2013, 27). Finally, the report estimated that lending for state capital financing could save $100 million in interest costs over 20 years. And the return from loans made by a public bank goes back to the state, and not to shareholders in other states and countries, keeping more of Vermont money local.

Notwithstanding the results of the economic impact analysis, the official recommendation to the legislature was just shy of endorsing a public bank. Instead, the report recommended an alternative approach that draws upon capacity that exists within existing lending agencies, especially the Vermont Economic Development Association (VEDA). Vermont's current economic development programs receive very high ratings on transparency and accountability from Good Jobs First, but a few large businesses have received substantial subsidies ("Accountable USA—Vermont" 2016). VEDA already had the capacity to function as a state depository, with assets comparable to those of the BND. Therefore, Vermont could charter VEDA as a bank and direct a larger portion of state funds to VEDA to lend. Then, over time, a VEDA bank could absorb more state deposits and expand the credit capacity of the state.

The legislature watered down the proposal, avoiding chartering VEDA as a bank. In 2014, after hearing testimony from dozens of witnesses, the Vermont legislature passed and the governor signed Vermont Act 199 (S. 220). The legislation created a [Vermont] Local Investment Advisory Committee (LIAC) within the Vermont Economic Development Authority (VEDA). LIAC was reauthorized in 2015 and again through July 1, 2018. A Vermont Entrepreneurial Lending Program was incorporated into the bill to allow lending to businesses that "have a demonstrable effect in achieving other public policy goals of the State, such as creating jobs in strategic sectors, location in a designated downtown, energy and thermal efficiency practices, or offering livable wage jobs" (Vermont Act 199, Sec. 4c).

In lieu of a state bank, the goal of LIAC is to increase economic development activity in Vermont and create jobs by committing up to 10% of the Treasurer's office average available cash in local investments. The first round of proposals was considered in early 2015. A second round was open until May 2016. Available funding was $3.75 million for housing, energy, and neighborhood revitalization projects and $350,000 for municipal infrastructure projects (Vermont LIAC 2016). Those eligible to apply for funds include municipalities, school districts, social services providers, state agencies and authorities, regional planning commissions, and similar organizations. All financing proposals and approvals are noted in LIAC minutes published by the Office of the State Treasurer. As examples, VEDA expended funds to invest in the following: child care subsidies to lower income households and jobs in the child care industry; renewable energy and energy efficiency; and new housing units. While not a full public bank, "[N]owhere have the steps toward public banking been more successful that in the state of Vermont. ... [Activists] combined savvy organizing with data-driven reports and policy briefs to prove the benefits of a public bank—like avoiding fat interest payments to Wall Street banks—for the state's economy" (Goldstein 2015).

A Revived Movement for Remedying the Problem of Social Balance

The long-term delegitimation of the state in the neoliberal era has caused skepticism about public debt—using borrowing for public investments—resulting in shortages of public funds and even necessitating emergency municipal borrowing at interest rates higher than the best rates for corporate customers. Deregulation of banking has led to mergers and acquisitions in financial services. Private sector banks are not grounded in their communities. Profit motives are not consistently directing credit toward activities that serve the public interest.

The revived public bank movement in the USA is still in its infancy. Further, it is operating in an environment where a mature private banking sector is a powerful vested interest, unlike when the Bank of North Dakota and public banks in other countries were founded. Because the Bank of North Dakota was created in a far different era and its existence has shaped the historical development of financial institutions in that state, it is a hard sell to simply push it as a model for other states to adopt wholesale. When only partisan players debate the pros and cons of public banks, policymakers may be reluctant to upset the status quo. Institutionalizing new public banks will, therefore, require a step-wise approach. Transitioning is likely to proceed incrementally, perhaps using the economic development authority route illustrated by the case study of Vermont.

A first stage is encouraging states to commission unbiased feasibility studies by credible scholars. These studies can document the gaps left by current private financial markets and public economic development initiatives and explore ways to move toward public banking that make sense in the local context. Local grassroots activists working with legislative champions and lobbyists on the ground can utilize the legitimacy of scholars and other experts, as none of these parties will succeed by working alone.

Contemporary advocates have seized upon an institutional model that pre-dates the neoliberal era and have updated it to address contemporary issues. Expanding beyond the mission of funding local economic development, today's movement also advances state-owned banks as a means of financing critical infrastructure investments. If states deposit their assets in their own banks, any surpluses can be redirected toward public goods and services. Public banking could become an important tool for remedying the problem of social balance identified by John Kenneth Galbraith.

Notes

1. For a history of public banking, see Brown (2013).
2. There is actually a long history of "development banks" in the U.S. In the 1780s, the Bank of New York, the Bank of Maryland, the Bank of Pennsylvania, and the First Bank of the United States were all organized to help finance local development projects. (I am indebted to Anne Mayhew for this insight.) According to Bray Hammond's history of U.S. banking from the American Revolution to the Civil War, the early American banking system was founded upon public banks (1957, Chap. 2).
3. BND neither works directly with private borrowers nor markets services to individuals, businesses, or local governments.

Supplementary Applications

1. View state legislature websites to search whether a public banking bill has been under consideration in your state or a neighboring state. Were hearings held on the bill? Who has testified for and against the bill? Can you summarize the arguments made?
2. Utilizing the Public Banking Institute website and other credible sources, find out what cities in the U.S. are currently considering a local/municipal public bank. Select a city and recap the progress made thus far.

References

Accountable USA—Vermont. 2016. *Good Jobs First.* http://www.goodjobsfirst.org/states/vermont.

American Society of Civil Engineers (ASCE). 2013. *Report Card for America's Infrastructure 2013*, March 2013. http://www.infrastructurereportcard.org/.

American Society of Civil Engineers (ASCE). 2017. *The Report Card for America's Infrastructure 2017*, March 2017. http://www.infrastructurereportcard.org/.

Brown, Ellen. 2014. *The Public Bank Solution.* Binzagr Institute for Sustainable Prosperity Policy Note No. 101, Granville, OH. http://www.binzagr-institute.org/policy-note-101/.

Brown, Ellen Hodgson. 2013. *The Public Bank Solution.* Baton Rouge, LA: Third Millennium Press.

Exploring a Public Bank for Vermont: Economic Impacts, Capital Needs, and Implementation. 2013, December. Vermonters for a New Economy, University of Vermont, and Political Economy Research Institute at the University of Massachusetts. http://lwvofvt.org/files/public_banking_1-13-2014.pdf.

Fettig, David. 1994. *Banking on the Government.* Minneapolis, MN: Federal Reserve Bank of Minneapolis. *The Region*, March. https://www.minneapolisfed.org/publications/the-region/banking-on-the-government.

Figart, Deborah M., and Mariam Majd. 2016. The Public Bank Movement: A Response to Local Economic Development and Infrastructure Needs in Three U.S. States. *Challenge* 59 (6): 461–479.

Fisher, Peter S. 1983. The Role of the Public Sector in Local Development Finance: Evaluating Alternative Institutional Arrangements. *Journal of Economic Issues* 17 (1): 133–153.

Galbraith, John Kenneth. 1958. *The Affluent Society*. Boston: Houghton-Mifflin.

Goldberg, Deb. Deb Goldberg Democrat for Treasurer Website. http://www.debgoldberg.com/visions-goals/.

Goldstein, Alexis. 2015. Vermonters Lobby for Public Bank—And Win Millions for Local Investment Instead, January 7. http://www.yesmagazine.org/commonomics/vermonters-lobby-public-bank-win-millions-for-local-investment.

Harkinson, Josh. 2009. How the Nation's Only State-Owned Bank Became the Envy of Wall Street. *Mother Jones*, March 27. http://www.motherjones.com/mojo/2009/03/how-nation%E2%80%99s-only-state-owned-bank-became-envy-wall-street.

Hammond, Bray. 1957. *Banks and Politics in America, from the Revolution to the Civil War*. Princeton, NJ: Princeton University Press.

Judd, Jason, and Heather McGhee. 2012. *Putting Money to Work for Vermont: Introducing the Vermont Partnership Bank*. Washington, DC: Dēmos.

Judd, Jason, and Sam Munger. 2010. *Building State Development Banks*. Madison, WI: Center for State Innovation. http://lwvofvt.org/files/buildingstatebanks.pdf.

Marois, Thomas. 2013. State-Owned Banks and Development: Dispelling Mainstream Myths. Queen's University Municipal Services Project Occasional Paper No. 2, December 2013, Kingston.

Mills, Karen Gordon, and Brayden McCarthy. 2014. The State of Small Business Lending: Credit access during the Recovery and How Technology May Change the Game. Harvard Business School Working Paper 15-004, July 22, Cambridge, MA.

Rapoport, Abby. 2013. The People's Bank. *The American Prospect*, April 1. http://prospect.org/article/people%E2%80%99s-bank-0.

Ratjan, Raghuram G., and Rodney Ramcharran. 2011. Land and Credit: A Study of the Political Economy of Banking in the United States in the Early 20th Century. *Journal of Finance* 66 (6): 1895–1931.

Schmitz, Janel. 2016. E-mail from BND Communications and Marketing Manager, July 22.

Schneiberg, Marc. 2013. Lost in Transposition? (A Cautionary Tale): The Bank of North Dakota and Prospects for Reform in American Banking. *Research in the Sociology of Organizations* 39A: 277–310.

[Vermont] Act 199. 2014. *An Act Relating To Furthering Economic Development*, June 24. http://legislature.vermont.gov/assets/Documents/2014/Docs/ACTS/ACT199/ACT199%20As%20Enacted.pdf.

[Vermont] Local Investment Advisory Committee (LIAC) Report. 2016. *LIAC report to the Vermont House and Senate*, January 12. Montpelier, VT. http://www.vermonttreasurer.gov/cash-investments/Local-Investment.

Vermont Legislative Joint Fiscal Office. 2010. Preliminary Review of Issues in Adopting a Bank of North Dakota (BND) Model in VT. Preliminary Issue Brief, January 2010, Vermont Legislative Joint Fiscal Office, Montpelier, VT.

von Mettenheim, Kurt. 2012. Public Banks: Competitive Advantages and Policy Alternatives. *Public Banking Institute Journal* 1 (1): 2–34.

Wiersch, Ann Marie. 2015. *Good News and Bad News on Small Business Lending in 2014*. Cleveland: Federal Reserve Bank of Cleveland. https://www.clevelandfed.org/newsroYourom-and-events/publications/community-development-briefs/db-20150105-good-news-bad-news-small-bus-lending.aspx.

Yeyati, Eduardo Levy, Alejandro Micco, and Ugo Panizza. 2007. A Reappraisal of State-Owned Banks. *Economia: Journal of the Latin American and Caribbean Economic Association* 7 (2): 209–247.

CHAPTER 4

Contesting the Gig Economy: #SchedulesThatWork

Abstract The old norms of the 9-to-5, 40-h workweek developed in the twentieth century have eroded. They have been replaced with unpredictable schedules where the number and timing of work hours can vary day-to-day. #SchedulesThatWork is a rallying cry for workers responding to this new flexibility. The chapter considers a new crusade for the nation's retail labor force, fueled by labor-worker–community coalitions such as the Retail Action Project. Led by New York State, several state attorneys general have sought to apply labor laws to curtail these employment practices. In a victory for their largely part-time workforce, some major retailers such as Starbucks, The Gap, Macys, and Zara have ended their "on-call" shifts and are posting schedules with more advance notice.

Keywords Irregular work schedules · Contingent work · Retail employment · Labor standards

JEL Codes J81 · J22 · L81

#SchedulesThatWork is a new rallying cry for workers responding to what companies call "flexibility" in the neoliberal era. Irregular work schedules with unpredictable or erratic work hours are a pivotal battleground in America's gig economy. Aided by sophisticated scheduling software such as timesheets.com, major retail employers have found a new way to cut costs and squeeze more out of their employees: they monitor demand and floor traffic, and call workers into duty only when needed—on little notice—and send them back home when business at the brick-and-mortar store slows. This employment practice is termed "just-in-time" scheduling. In a victory for their largely part-time workforce (and workers' family lives), the following retailers in the USA have taken steps to end their "on-call" shift schedules for employees: The Gap (and its brands Old Navy, Banana Republic, Athleta, Intemic), Abercrombie & Fitch, Victoria's Secret, J. Crew, Urban Outfitters, T.J. Maxx, JCPenney, Zara, Williams-Sonoma, and Target. So has Starbucks for its 130,000 baristas nationwide. As former US Secretary of Labor Robert Reich (2015) has said, "All the blather about 'family-friendly workplaces' is meaningless if workers have no control over when they're working. … American workers can't simultaneously be variable costs for businesses yet live in their own fixed-cost worlds."

But workers are fighting back. Powerful personal stories have played out in social media and on the front pages of newspapers and news magazines, forcing retail employers to back down from employment practices that treat employees as disposable commodities. One compelling example was the story of Jannette Navarro, a single mother who is a barista at Starbucks, published in the *New York Times* in 2014. Navarro told reporter Jodi Kantor that irregular hours had turned her life into a "chronic chaos over the clock." Her job controlled other aspects of her life—how much and when she and her child slept and what groceries and bills she could afford each week. One Friday, July 4 (Independence Day), she was scheduled to work until 11:00 pm, then to report just 5 h later, on Saturday (a practice called "clopening"); her third shift in a 2-day period was at 5:00 am on Sunday morning. Just one day after the stirring article about Navarro, Starbucks announced it would seek to improve its scheduling practices (Kantor 2014a, b, August 13 and 14; see also Lam 2015; Reich 2015; Scheiber 2015; Schneider 2015; Weber 2015).

In addition to telling their stories through traditional media, activists have utilized social media, including tweets with hashtags, as a means of spreading a message, identifying potential allies, and exerting moral suasion on employers. Retail workers and their allies have roused a movement with the Twitter hashtags #SchedulesThatWork and #JustHours. This new crusade for economic justice for the nation's retail labor force has been fueled by labor-worker–community coalitions such as the Retail Action Project, retail worker unions, and advocates for family-friendly policies. In addition, several state attorneys general, especially Eric T. Schneiderman in New York State, have sought to apply labor laws to curtail these employment practices.

THE PRONOUNCED RISE OF PRECARIOUS WORK

The trend toward labor flexibility in its various guises is not new, nor is it unique to the United States. In his presidential address to the American Sociological Association, Arne Kalleberg observed that precarious work has become increasingly widespread in the USA, Europe, and Canada. Precarious work is "employment that is uncertain, unpredictable, and risky from the point of view of the worker" (Kalleberg 2009, 2). Guy Standing (2011) terms the growth of this new class of workers "the precariat." Increasingly, the labor markets in advanced industrial nations resemble a gig economy. Think of series of live band performances in various cities, a sequence of gigs. Uber drivers, Lyft drivers, TaskRabbit or Thumbtack.com fillers, and millions of service workers have short-term gigs rather than long-term, steady, full-time employment. Like struggling musicians, they cobble together income with no guarantee of economic security.

Manufacturing employers developed just-in-time production techniques in the 1980s. Walmart, America's largest retailer, pioneered just-in-time inventory management (supply system) in the 1990s. In the new century, the corporate fetish with flexibility to drive down costs has migrated to employment rolls, with part-time or temporary or contingent or contract jobs evolving into just-in-time scheduling practices (Alexander et al. 2015; Boushey and Ansel 2016). Today, employers not only manage the overall number of workers but their units of time, in ever-smaller timesheet units—even 15 mins at a time!

Since 2006, major retailers have transformed their hiring practices. One oft-cited empirical study involving semi-structured interviews with staff at 22 work sites in four industries, including retail, is by Susan Lambert from the University of Chicago. According to Lambert: "Retail provides the best example of how accountability practices influence the extent to which instability is transferred to workers. In all the retail stores studied, managers were held accountable for maintaining a particular ratio between the number of hours employees worked and either store sales or traffic," a payroll hours-to-sales ratio (Lambert 2008, 1212). "Corporate" and/or higher level managers, Lambert continues, review the ratios daily and managers are expected to rebalance by the next week or next day. In one particularly bad extreme, a retailer monitored the labor-to-sales ratio hourly and staffing adjustments were made throughout the day. Yet the irony is that these systems do not necessarily work as efficiently as the hype (see, for example, "Taming Scheduling Software" 2014). Perfect sales forecasts do not exist. In fact, the relationship between utilizing flexible labor and resultant financial performance has been found to have an inverted U-shape (Kesavan et al. 2014).

In the pursuit of flexibility, a largely full-time retail workforce has been flipped into a part-time workforce; at least 70% of jobs are part-time. The amount of underwork—the number of employees working fewer hours than they wished—is at an all-time high (Alexander and Haley-Lock 2015). Even full-time employment status does not guarantee full-time hours on a regular weekly basis. Further, in low-level hourly jobs in the USA, some other type of flexibility is going on. "Whether in small, independent establishments or large, national firms, pressures to 'stay within hours' result in managers feeling constrained in the total number of hours they distribute among their staff and, in turn, in their ability to respond to workers' hour and schedule preferences" (Lambert et al. 2012, 296). One study of retail workers in New York City reveals that only 17% have a set schedule (Luce and Fujita 2012). Another study from the Economic Policy Institute by economist Lonnie Golden (2015) estimates that about 15% of sales and related occupations have irregular or on-call schedules; based upon his measurement methodology, this percentage, he adds, is likely a lower bound estimate.

What happens in retail matters. It is a large and growing industry. In the USA, the retail industry employs roughly 16 million employees, about 10% of the labor force. Despite the growth of online sales, jobs are projected to rise at least as fast as average by 2024 (Aspen Institute n.d.; U.S. Bureau of Labor Statistics 2015).[1] The most common job titles are cashier and retail salesperson. Retail workers are evenly divided among men and women, disproportionately people of color, and tend to skew younger in age. Jobs are low paid; in 2015, the median wage was only $10.60 per hour for retail sales workers. Retail sales work is part of the precariat, predominantly part-time and without benefits.

Trends in retail also have important implications for other industries. According to a variety of estimates, the size of the contingent labor force has grown in the last decade. In 2005, for the first time, the U.S. Bureau of Labor Statistics (BLS) included a Contingent Work Supplement

(CWS) to the Current Population Survey. More current national data about alternative work arrangements are not readily available since the CWS has not been repeated. Relying on other surveys for updated estimates, researchers and policy makers have found that, depending on the definition, the size of the contingent workforce ranges from 5% to more than one-third of the entire US labor force. Just one core group of agency temporary workers and on-call workers comprised 7.9% of the labor force in 2010 (U.S. GAO 2015). A more recent Rand-Princeton Contingent Work Survey by Economists Lawrence Katz and Alan Krueger (2016) finds a significant rise from 10.1% in 2005 to 15.8% in 2015. Katz and Krueger (2016) assert: "A striking implication of these estimates is that all of the net employment growth in the U.S. economy from 2005 to 2015 appears to have occurred in alternative work arrangements" (7). They define alternative work as temporary help agency workers, on-call workers, contract workers, and independent contractors or freelancers; but available data likely underestimate the problem of on-call workers because of how the questions are phrased (see Lambert 2008).

America's employment laws and regulations provide no antidote for underwork caused by unpredictable work schedules. In the United States, the norm of a full-time 40-h workweek—after which hourly workers would be entitled to overtime—has been governed by the Fair Labor Standards Act (FLSA) since 1938. While not mandating a 40-h workweek, the overtime rule, along with union contracts in dominant industries, institutionalized the concept of a full-time job for the latter half of the twentieth century. This social norm, as well as other dimensions of employment relations, is in a process of unraveling.

In fact, it is the (mal)*distribution* of hours across the work week that is a paramount problem for today's working families. In terms of hours, it is a tale of two different worlds. Increasingly, there are overworked Americans—long hours and mandatory overtime—among the professional and managerial class and underwork among the near poor (Golden and Figart 2000; Golden and Wiens-Tuers 2005; Kalleberg 2007). The combination of overwork for some and underwork for others has gendered dimensions, as employees with family responsibilities are overly crowded into relatively low-paid, short-hour jobs. Contingent workers are likely to be: younger, people of color, women, single parents, and persons with limited education and skills, i.e., who possess only a high school diploma (see, for example, McCrate 2012; Lambert et al.

2012, 2014; Luce and Fujita 2012; Golden 2015). The institutional norm of full-time employment is changing, but not in a progressive direction.

Flexibility for Whom? Workers Take on Big Retail

Today, many hourly workers, especially those in retail, are sent home early or called in at the last minute. It is not unusual for a retail worker to check her schedule online 1 h or less before heading to the subway station or to receive a text message from an employer saying she is not needed within the next hour or two. What should she do? She is obviously out of the expected income even though she has already arranged for childcare, the expected expense. She cannot challenge the employer's scheduling software.

The unpredictable and variable work schedules make it hard to build a life. Among the challenges are balancing work and family, caring for children, running errands, heading to after-work and community activities, volunteering, going to the doctor, planning a dinner or movie with friends, getting enough sleep and exercise, and even taking a second job. Irregular hours also mean unpredictable paychecks. Variable hours make it hard to maintain a household budget and save money. One week's savings can be wiped away by the next week's underwork. Unfortunately, neither the FLSA nor any other federal law provides any remedy for the insecurity associated with erratic work schedules. While there is a legally mandated minimum wage per hour, there are no minimum hours. There is no protection for underwork.[2]

New York City has been a key location for the organized response to on-call scheduling. Some retail workers in large department stores are already unionized, their contracts with progressive employment practices providing models for others. Out of this fertile ground sprang the New York City-based Retail Action Project (RAP), an advocacy organization working for better labor standards in the retail industry. RAP (at http://retailactionproject.org) was founded in 2005 as a community–labor partnership between the Retail, Wholesale and Department Store Union (RWDSU) of the United Food and Commercial Workers (UFCW) and a community housing organization on the lower east side. It expanded into a voluntary member-run non-profit organization in 2010.[3] RAP helps New York City retail workers know their rights through education campaigns, particularly in order to fight wage theft and underemployment. As one of RAP's worker-members explains: "At RAP we work to improve retail jobs through organizing, media and policy" (quoted in Ikeler 2014, 113).

RAP debuted its Just Hours campaign in 2012 in response to employer scheduling tactics. Worker-members have picketed outside New York Fashion Week events, delivered petitions to management through grassroots action in retail stores, and used social media and mainstream media to promote their message. They used the hashtag #JustHours in their protests outside the Abercrombie & Fitch flagship store in 2012 and Juicy Couture in 2013. A prominent #ChangeZara campaign is aimed at Zara (parent company is Intertext), a clothing retailer headquartered in Spain; on July 29, 2014, workers in New York City protested. Their goal: the same guaranteed access to benefits and representation as Zara workers across the Atlantic.

Scholarship in the social sciences can be crucial for the worker campaigns, lending credibility and support. In 2012, RAP co-published what is a now a valued study of retail workers (non-managers). *Discounted Jobs: How Retailers Sell Workers Short* is based on face-to-face surveys with 436 workers, followed by focus groups. Authors Stephanie Luce and Naoki Fujita (2012) provide a comprehensive picture of retail employees in New York City.

Low wages and involuntary part-time employment were expected outcomes. What seemed to bubble to the surface were the accounts of work schedules. Only half of those surveyed know of their work schedule within a week. About one in five only gets 3-day notice. And one in five workers must always or often be available for "on-call" shifts; workers are expected to call the store the morning of the shift or the night before. This happens several days a week. One-third of workers surveyed said that they were sometimes, often, or very often sent home early. And there is considerable "off the clock" work. One worker at Banana Republic divulged to the researchers: "My schedule was always posted at the last minute, sometimes only 2 or 3 days in advance. On top of that, they frequently changed the schedule but wouldn't notify anyone. Sometimes I would miss a shift because I had been rescheduled, but even though I was not informed I would still get in trouble" (Luce and Fujita 2012, 8).

In a second study titled *Short Shifted*, the authors (Luce et al. 2016) surveyed over 200 workers in the boroughs of Manhattan and Brooklyn, focusing on those workers employed by national apparel stores.

The researchers followed up by conducting in-depth interviews with 44 survey respondents. *Short Shifted* features worker daily experiences—their actual lives on and off the job—and the effect of living with unstable work hours. Retail workers cannot control their hours, the authors find, making it difficult for families:

> Almost all of the workers we interviewed grapple with unpredictable schedules, misused technology, part-time limbo, arbitrary rules, favoritism, barriers to a career ladder, or wage theft, as well as the challenges of balancing work, child care, and school. Only 40 percent of workers surveyed have set minimum hours per week, and approximately half of the part-time workers we surveyed would like to work full-time. One quarter of the workers are scheduled for on-call shifts, and the vast majority report that they find out from a supervisor if they are needed for the on-call shift only two hours before the shift starts. (Luce et al. 2016, 4)

Researchers are doing more than documenting problems. Funded by the Washington Center for Equitable Growth, Joan Williams and Susan Lambert of the Center for WorkLife Law at Hastings College of Law are working in partnership with Gap, Inc. to create and test a more worker- and manager-friendly pilot program to stabilize worker schedules. Their ongoing study is designed to compare stores with and without the pilot program. Gap Inc. is cooperating as part of its commitment to end on-call shifts globally, announced in its 2013–2014 global sustainability report (Gap Inc. 2013–2014). Their actions are indicative of a recognition by some companies that retailers that guarantee a minimum number of hours at higher rates of pay and better benefits have lower turnover costs, as corroborated by several studies by management professors (see Cascio 2006; Ton 2012).

Enlisting the Help of Government Actors

New York has also been a center of activism in the area of proactive public policy because it is one of a few states that has pre-existing legislation facilitating legal challenges to just-in-time scheduling. By 2016, seven US states (California, Connecticut, Massachusetts, New Hampshire, New Jersey, New York and Rhode Island) and Washington, DC had "reporting pay" or "show-up pay" laws. (Oregon, too, has legislation, but it only applies to workers under 18 years of age.) Reporting pay laws require employers to pay workers for a minimum number of hours of a scheduled shift, whether worked or not. Modeled after provisions in union contracts, these laws help steady income with guaranteed employment hours. Government officials in a number of states have utilized the threat of enforcing these reporting pay laws to get companies to agree to alter their scheduling practices.

The leader in utilizing the enforcement teeth of reporting pay has been New York State Attorney General Eric T. Schneiderman. On April 10, 2014, Schneiderman's labor bureau chief sent letters to thirteen retailers, releasing them to the *Wall Street Journal*. The letters, archived by the *Journal* (see Weber 2015), expressed concern about the effect of "on-call" shifts on workers and their families, requested information, and reminded companies that when an employee reports for a scheduled shift, New York State law requires that they be paid for at least 4 h (or the number of hours in the regular shift), at the basic minimum hourly wage. The second paragraph of the letter states:

> Our office has received reports that a growing number of employers, particularly in the retail industry, require their hourly workers to work what are sometimes known as "on-call shifts"—that is, requiring their employees to call into work just a few hours in advance, or the night before, to determine whether the worker needs to appear for work that day or the next. If the employee is told that his or her services are not needed, the employee will receive no pay for that day, despite being required to be available to appear on the job site the next day or even just a few hours later on the same day. For many workers, that is too little time to make arrangements for family needs, let alone to find an alternative source of income to compensate for the lost pay. (New York State, Office of the Attorney General, letter to Gap Inc. 2014)

The Attorney General's Office sent similar letters to a number of retailers in 2015 and 2016. The Retail Action Project developed a tool to help employees keep track of their hours to help document possible labor law violations investigated by Attorney General Schneiderman's office. It is called "The Scheduling Handbook" and is available online (see RAP n.d.). The letters in New York refer to earlier letters and conversations with retailers that have led companies to stop using "on-call" scheduling practices nationwide and agree to post employee work schedules at least one week prior to the start of the workweek. The initiative is spreading. In 2016, the state attorneys general from the seven states and Washington, D.C. with reporting pay laws followed New York's example and sent letters to retailers in their states (New York State, Office of the Attorney General 2016).

Local and federal legislation to tackle on-call scheduling has also been enacted or proposed.[4] In 2013, the City of San Francisco passed a family-friendly workplace ordinance that allows employees the right to request flexible work arrangements, without retaliation for asking. San Francisco is a "propitious site" for protecting worker rights due to a number of factors discussed by Miriam Wells (2014, 267). That same city where Gap Inc. has its headquarters went further to regulate hours, retention, scheduling, and treatment of part-time employees at covered retail establishments. Two companion "Formula Retail Employee Rights Ordinances" require retailers to provide a good faith estimate of a reasonable number of hours/shifts per month, posting work schedules with advance notice, give "predictability pay" for sudden changes in a work schedule, and pay for on-call shifts for workers in the retail industry. The ordinances passed on November 25, 2014, became operative on October 3, 2015, and the final implementing rules took effect March 1, 2016. As the first legislation of its kind for retail workers, these "Retail Workers Bill of Rights" ordinances serve as a model for other cities (and the USA) that have introduced similar legislation.

State and local campaigns around minimum wage hikes, paid sick leave, and family leave have served as models for federal legislation. With resounding support from activists and policy advocates such as the Retail Action Project, the National Women's Law Center, Jobs with Justice, CLASP, Center for Popular Democracy, the National Partnership for Women & Families, and the United Food and Commercial Workers Union, Senator Elizabeth Warren (D-MA) and Representative Rosa DeLauro (D-CT) introduced the Schedules That Work Act (S. 1772) in the 114th US Congress in 2015. This legislation would grant workers at firms with 15 or more employees the right to request a flexible work schedule, with protection from retaliation. The proposed bill also requires reporting pay and call-in pay and necessitates advance notice of work schedules, at least 14 days in advance. The National Partnership for Women & Families (2015) argues that passage of the bill is part of a multi-faceted strategy to reduce the gender-based wage gap because it helps women have the income stability needed to remain on the job and advance on the job. The bill faces an uphill battle against the National

Retail Federation lobby group and remained stuck in committee late in 2016.

Shifting Norms on Shift Work

The institutional norms of the late twentieth century regarding work schedules have eroded. Although the old norms of the 9-to-5, 40-h workweek were problematic for employees with family responsibilities, unpredictable schedules have been an even more regressive turn. Retail workers are fighting back against the flexibility driven solely by employer needs, challenging this race to the bottom. They have worked in coalition with unions, community organizations, feminist advocates, and political institutions to pressure employers. The goal is a new set of institutionalized employment practices that eliminate invidious distinctions between "the precariat" and traditional employees.

Campaigns such as SchedulesThatWork, JustHours, and the Fair Workweek Initiative, in conjunction with tough enforcement of labor regulations and union negotiations at organized workplaces, have forced employers to take action to improve their scheduling policies and practices. In addition to the successes noted at the outset of this chapter, retailers now taking the high road and providing stable employment scheduling include Macys, Bloomingdale's, Costco, Trader Joe's, Quik Trip, and Borders. One element of this pressure is workers telling their stories via social and traditional media, to make their challenges tangible to others. Retail employers are particularly vulnerable to such strategies; image to their customers is critical to their bottom line.

Notes

1. A similar portrait of retail employment is presented globally (see Carré et al. 2010).
2. The negative effects of irregular work hours on families, children, and employees themselves are exacting and strongly associated with gender. For a discussion of the research, see McCrate (2012), Ton (2012), Henly and Lambert (2014), Golden (2015), McCrate (2016), and Vogtman and Schulman (2016).
3. A history of RAP's formation is found in Ikeler (2014).
4. My summary of legislation here is drawn from the following sources: City of San Francisco (2013), City of San Francisco (n.d.), Alexander et al.

(2015), Golden (2015), National Women's Law Center (2015), and Boushey (2016).

Supplementary Application

1. An interactive website designed to illuminate the struggles of retail workers can be found at https://clockingin.raceforward.org/. Go to the website and click on one of the three industries and put yourself in the shoes of an employee. If you have your own experiences in retail or another service sector job, compare these stories with your own experiences.

References

Alexander, Charlotte, and Anna Haley-Lock. 2015. Underwork, Work-Hour Insecurity, and a New Approach to Wage and Hour Regulation. *Industrial Relations* 54 (4): 695–716.

Alexander, Charlotte, Anna Haley-Lock, and Nantiya Ruan. 2015. Stabilizing Low-Wage Work. *Harvard Civil Rights-Civil Liberties Law Review* 50 (1): 1–48.

Aspen Institute. n.d. Profiles of the Retail Workforce and the Retail Action Project. http://www.aspenwsi.org/wordpress/wp-content/uploads/Profiles-of-the-Retail-Workforce-and-the-Retail-Action-Project.pdf.

Boushey, Heather. 2016. *Finding Time: The Economics of Work-Life Conflict*. Cambridge: Harvard University Press.

Boushey, Heather, and Bridget Ansel. 2016. *Working by the Hour: The Economic Consequences of Unpredictable Scheduling Practices*. Washington, DC: Washington Center for Equitable Growth.

Carré Françoise, Chris Tilly, Maarten Van Klaveren, and Dorothea Voss-Dahm. 2010. Retail Jobs in Comparative Perspective. In *Low-Wage Work in the Wealthy World*, ed. Jérôme Gautié and John Schmitt, 211–268. New York: Russell Sage Foundation.

Cascio, Wayne F. 2006. Decency Means More than 'Always Low Prices': A Comparison of Costco to Wal-Mart's Sam's Club. *Academy of Management Perspectives* 20 (3): 26–37.

City of San Francisco. Formula Retail Employee Rights Ordinances. http://sfgov.org/olse/formula-retail-employee-rights-ordinances.

City of San Francisco is Family Friendly Workplace Ordinance, No. 209-13. 2013. http://sfgov.org/olse/FAMILY-FRIENDLY-WORKPLACE-ORDINANCE-FFWO.

Gap Inc. 2013–2014. *Our Futures Are Woven Together: Global Sustainability Report 2013–2014.* http://www.gapincsustainability.com/sites/default/files/Gap%20Inc.%202013%20-%2014%20Report.pdf.

Golden, Lonnie. 2015. Irregular Work Scheduling and its Consequences. EPI Briefing Paper #394, Washington, DC.

Golden, Lonnie, and Deborah M. Figart (eds.). 2000. *Working Time: International Trends, Theory, and Policy.* London: Routledge.

Golden, Lonnie, and Barbara Wiens-Tuers. 2005. Mandatory Overtime Work in the United States: Who, Where, and What? *Labor Studies Journal* 30 (1): 1–25.

Henly, Julia R., and Susan J. Lambert. 2014. Unpredictable Work Timing in Retail Jobs: Implications for Employee Work-Life Conflict. *Industrial and Labor Relations Review* 67 (3): 986–1016.

Ikeler, Peter. 2014. Infusing Craft Identity into a Noncraft Industry: The Retail Action Project. In *New Labor in New York: Precarious Workers and the Future of the Labor Movement*, ed. Ruth Milkman and Ed Ott, 113–133. Ithaca, NY: Cornell University Press/ILR Press.

Kantor, Jodi. 2014a. Working Anything but 9 to 5. *New York Times*, August 13.

Kantor, Jodi. 2014b. Starbucks to Revise Policies to End Irregular Schedules for Its 130,000 Baristas. *New York Times*, August 14.

Katz, Lawrence F., and Alan B. Krueger. 2016. The Rise and Nature of Alternative Work Arrangements in the United States, 1995–2015. Working Paper, March 29, 2016.

Kalleberg, Arne L. 2007. *The Mismatched Worker.* New York: W.W. Norton.

Kalleberg, Arne L. 2009. Precarious Work, Insecure Workers: Employment Relations in Transition. *American Sociological Review* 74 (1): 1–22.

Kesavan, Saravanan, Bradley R. Staats, and Wendell Gilland. 2014. Volume Flexibility in Services: The Costs and Benefits of Flexible Labor Resources. *Management Science* 60 (8): 1884–1906.

Lam, Bourree. 2015. The End of On-Call Scheduling? *The Atlantic*, October 23.

Lambert, Susan J. 2008. Passing the Buck: Labor Flexibility Practices that Transfer Risk onto Hourly Workers. *Human Relations* 91 (9): 1203–1227.

Lambert, Susan J., Peter J. Fugiel, and Julia R. Henly. 2014. *Precarious Work Schedules Among Early-Career Employees in the US: A National Snapshot.* EINet Report. Chicago, IL. (EINet Report). https://ssascholars.uchicago.edu/einet/working-papers.

Lambert, Susan J., Anna Haley-Lock, and Julia R. Henly. 2012. Schedule Flexibility in Hourly Jobs: Unanticipated Consequences and Promising Directions. *Community, Work & Family* 15 (3): 293–315.

Luce, Stephanie, and Naoki Fujita. 2012. *Discounted Jobs: How Retailers Sell Workers Short.* New York: Murphy Institute, City University of New York, and the Retail Action Project.

Luce, Stephanie, Sasha Hammad, and Darrah Sipe. 2016. *Short Shifted*. New York: Murphy Institute of the City University of New York and Retail, Wholesale and Department Store Union. http://retailactionproject.org/2014/09/short-shifted/.

McCrate, Elaine. 2012. Flexibility for Whom? Control Over Work Schedule Variability in the US. *Feminist Economics* 18 (1): 1–34.

McCrate, Elaine. 2016. Unstable Scheduling, Precarious Employment, and Gender. EINet Working Paper, University of Chicago, Chicago, IL. https://ssascholars.uchicago.edu/einet/working-papers.

National Partnership for Women & Families. 2015. *An Unlevel Playing Field: America's Gender-Based Pay Gap, Binds of Discrimination, and a Path Forward*. Issue Brief, April 2015. Washington, DC.

National Women's Law Center. 2015. *Recently Introduced and Enacted State and Local Fair Scheduling Legislation*. Washington, DC. https://nwlc.org/state-by-state/.

New York State, Office of the Attorney General. 2014. Letters and Press Releases About On-Call Scheduling. Available from the *Wall Street Journal* at http://online.wsj.com/public/resources/documents/laborletter.pdf.

New York State, Office of the Attorney General. 2016. A.G. Schneiderman and Eight Other State Attorneys General Probe Retailers Overuse of On-Call Shifts. April 13. http://www.ag.ny.gov/press-release/ag-schneiderman-and-eight-other-state-attorneys-general-probe-retailers-over-use-call.

Reich, Robert. 2015. How Flexible Scheduling Is Making American Workers' Lives Miserable. *In These Times*, April 24.

Retail Action Project. Track Your Hours. http://retailactionproject.org/campaigns-2/sustainable-scheduling-new/track-your-hours/.

Scheiber, Noam. 2015. The Perils of Ever-Changing Work Schedules Extend to Children's Well-Being. *New York Times*, August 12.

Schneider, Nathan. 2015. End of the 8-Hour Day? *The Nation*, May 11, 13–16.

Standing, Guy. 2011. *The Precariat: The New Dangerous Class*. London: Bloomsbury Academic.

Taming Scheduling Software. 2014. *Harvard Business Review* 92 (12): 34.

Ton, Zeynep. 2012. Why 'Good Jobs' Are Good for Retailers. *Harvard Business Review* 90 (1/2): 124–131.

U.S. Bureau of Labor Statistics. 2015. Retail Sales Workers. *Summary*. http://www.bls.gov/ooh/sales/retail-sales-workers.htm.

U.S. Government Accountability Office (GAO). 2015. *Contingent Workforce: Size, Characteristics, Earnings, and Benefits*. Washington, DC (GAO-15-168R).

Vogtman, Julie, and Karen Schulman. 2016. *Set Up to Fail: When Low-Wage Work Jeopardizes Parents' and Children's Success*. Washington, DC: National Women's Law Center.

Weber, Lauren. 2015. Retailers Are Under Fire for Work Schedules. *Wall Street Journal*, April 12.

Wells, Miriam J. 2014. Labor Policy and Local Economic Development. In *When Mandates Work: Raising Labor Standards at the Local Level*, ed. Michael Reich, Ken Jacobs, and Miranda Dietz, 256–285. Berkeley: University of California Press.

CHAPTER 5

Delving into the Food Supply Chain: The Case of Fresh Tomatoes

Abstract This story opens in Immokalee, Florida, the fresh tomato capital of the USA. It is about one aspect of social practices in food production: the movement to increase the pay of farmworkers in the supply chain of the American tomato. In a new model of worker organizing, the Coalition of Immokalee Workers (CIW) realized growers were themselves squeezed by large fast food companies and supermarkets. So the Coalition went directly to food giants through their "penny a pound" movement, demanding that companies sign a Fair Food Agreement with a human rights code of conduct and independent monitoring. Today, coast to coast, at many fast food restaurants in the USA, you are eating a fair food tomato. And tomato pickers are earning more per week.

Keywords Labor rights · Migrant workers · Agricultural sector Boycotts · Supply chains · Fair trade · Social movements

JEL Codes J31 · J43 · J61 · J81 · L66 · Q1

Millions of Americans, like me, are "foodies." We enjoy dining out, trying new recipes at home, tending to our private or community gardens, and—increasingly—visiting farmers markets to buy more local organic or sustainable food, and food from farms that treat animals with care. We are part of the alternative food movement concerned with the ethical implications of our consumption decisions. Yet, with few exceptions, our interest in the food we consume, popularized by visual media and critics, has tended to overlook the working conditions of the largely non-citizen, migrant, undocumented workers who toil to bring us our food. When we watch reality television shows such as Top Chef, the visual images of the food preparation and dining, and even twists envisioned by producers—having chefs go into the fields to pick crops or donning waders to go clamming—rarely address the actual conditions in the fields or seas. This is particularly surprising because 40 years ago, the United Farm Workers union (UFW), led by Cesar Chavez, was one of the first social movements to engage Americans in the politics of food production.

An exception is the 2014 documentary movie, *Food Chains*.[1] The movie opens in the town of Immokalee, Florida, the tomato capital of the United States at sunrise. The camera pans across dusty streets, ramshackle buildings, and a warehouse of a vegetable packing service named Tomato Man, Inc. At 4:30 am, 15–16 tomato pickers and their families in trailers are waking up from mattresses stacked end-to-end on the floor of a trailer, heating coffee on something that looks like a stove from a junkyard, sharing an overcrowded and unsanitary half bathroom, dragging their young children from their slumber to a babysitter, all in hurried fashion so they do not miss the 5:00 am bus to the fields. "We live like animals in cramped houses," says one worker. Poor wages and working conditions predominate in large agribusiness and small farms alike, from Florida to California to the wealthy suburbs of cities like New York (Gray 2014).

This story of institutional change is about one aspect of social practices in food production: the movement to increase the pay of farmworkers in the supply chain of the American tomato. Supply chains are an evolving institution in the contemporary political economy, representing a shift in power from producers to those who distribute goods and services. Successful strategies for forging progressive institutional change, therefore, are different today than several decades ago, reflecting these changes in economic structures. In this example, a different form of worker organization has evolved to bring about change.

American Fresh Tomatoes and the Farmworkers Who Pick Them

I was inspired to research this story after viewing *Food Chains* and reading an exposé by former *Gourmet* magazine writer Barry Estabrook (2009), followed by a longer discussion in his book, *Tomatoland* (2012). In the USA, tomatoes are the second most popular vegetable behind lettuce (although, as we all know, they are technically fruit). The USA is a leading world producer of tomatoes, second only to China. Fresh and processed tomatoes amount to about $2 billion of annual farm cash receipts. Although grown in every US state, California and Florida together provide about two-thirds of the acreage for the crop. Fresh tomatoes in Florida (unlike tomatoes for canning in California) are still picked individually by hand. This story about the tomato workers has a happy, though still evolving, ending.[2]

Starting in a basement of a Catholic Church in 1993, the Coalition of Immokalee Workers (CIW) is perhaps the best known movement to combat farmworker exploitation since the United Farm Workers union (UFW), and it is the winner of many human rights awards and prizes. This coalition brings together workers and faith-based groups, student activists, and other progressives. Their innovative strategy has resulted in average wage increases of about 25%, with some workers doubling their daily wages.

Unlike the UFW, the CIW did not attempt the daunting task of organizing the panoply of migrant field hands across multiple employers into a labor union. The tomato pickers are immigrants mostly from Mexico, Guatemala, and Haiti, but also from other parts of Central and South America, too. As many as a dozen or so languages are spoken in the tomato fields. Day workers gather each morning in a parking lot on Immokalee to be taken to the fields for the day. CIW member Greg Asbed (2007, 6) says: "It is an employer's dream, and an organizer's nightmare."

The strategic change—from union to coalition—reflects the relative economic power of retailers over producers in today's economy. CIW realized that tomato growers were themselves squeezed by American's largest fast food companies and supermarkets. Walmart had a long history of pressure on its suppliers. As the chain increased its market share in the retail food industry, the supermarket industry followed suit to cut costs and squeeze out more profits by increasing concentration/

oligopolization—that is, ownership by just a few firms—and putting downward pressure on prices and costs of production. So the Coalition of Immokalee Workers went directly to the retailers and, through their "penny a pound" movement, began to secure higher wages for seasonal, mostly migrant, tomato pickers. Justin Miller (2015) calls these "alt-labor" organizing efforts. Instead of focusing on organizing to confront direct employers, these movements acknowledge the complexity of global supply chains and the precariousness of labor relations today.

Farmworkers were originally excluded from the Fair Labor Standards Act of 1938, the law that set the nation's first minimum wage because southern votes were needed for passage and farm labor lacked the political clout of industrial unions. Technically, since the 1966 amendments, farmworkers *paid hourly* must earn the minimum. In reality, coverage is limited. Loopholes are exploited and enforcement is poor. *Piece rate work*, like picking bushel-sized baskets of tomatoes, is still exempt from the minimum wage. And seasonal work in growing and harvesting periods is intermixed with unemployment spells. According to the U.S. Department of Labor's National Agriculture Workers Survey (NAWS), the average wage rate of today's hired farmworkers is $10.80 per hour in 2012 dollars (U.S. Department of Agriculture 2016). Annually, this is typically only about $12,000 per year because the work is seasonal.

CIW co-founder Lucas Benitez is originally from Mexico and immigrated to the USA with his family to work the fields. In *Fair Food*, Oran B. Hesterman narrates his visit to Immokalee and the tour that Lucas Benitez took him on: "He strategically ended our tour in the dusty parking lot and pointed to one of the rusted singlewide trailers, asking me to consider the number of shoes out front. I counted 14 pairs. More than a dozen men lived in that trailer, with a single hot plate, one small bathroom, and fourteen mattresses lining the floor. For this, they each paid $100 per month, meaning that the monthly rent for the trailer came to $1400" (Hesterman 2011, 63).

An assistant attorney once called south Florida's tomato fields "ground zero for modern-day slavery" (quoted in Estabrook 2012, xix). In *The Slave Next Door*, Kevin Bales and Ron Soodalter write: "Picking tomatoes is brutal; it requires working bent over in the southern sun for hours on end straightening only long enough to run 100–150 ft with a filled 32 lb bucket and literally throw it up to the worker on the truck. Lunch is a hurried affair, and water breaks are few" (2010:

45). Health risks include exposure to chemicals, dehydration and heat stroke, and lack access to clean drinking and bathing water. As depicted in *Food Chains*, Immokalee workers pick up to 4000 lb of tomatoes per ten-to-twelve-hour day, earning about $40, or an average of 1 penny per pound. One worker relates, "You have to work like a freak to make enough money so your family can eat" (quoted in Estabrook 2012, 99). Workers do not earn overtime and are not covered by health insurance or any other benefits.

The CIW has led an anti-slavery campaign since the 1990s. The supply chain strategy evolved out of early failures. Going after the growers to improve wages proved to be difficult. The growers would not budge, so CIW decided to follow the trail of the tomatoes once they left the field. CIW learned that growers themselves were squeezed to sell tomatoes cheaper and cheaper by large restaurant and supermarket chains. Downward pressure on prices led to downward pressure on wages. CIW member Greg Asbed argues: "If further gains for human rights in Florida's agricultural industry were to be won, workers in Immokalee would have to locate the growers' Achilles heel, the one unprotected point of entry in their armor, to press their campaign and win further improvements in their lives" (2007, 18). Supermarkets operate as virtual monopolies, dictating the prices down the supply chain. "They are the price *setters*, not price *takers*" (Bales and Soodalter 2010, 48, emphasis original). Supermarkets and fast food chains indirectly push workers to work longer for less pay. As Benitez exclaims, "[t]hey are creating the poverty of Immokalee!"

CONFRONT THE END USER (FOOD GIANTS): A NEW MODEL OF ORGANIZING

In the 2000s, CIW built a novel model of labor relations that Katherine Caldwell (2011), Director of the Human Right to Work with Dignity Program, says directly confronts the private actors/companies which profit from the poverty of exploited workers. The CIW worker organization model is based on progressive movements in the Caribbean as well as Central and South America (e.g., the Zapatista movement and/or liberation theology), precisely where the tomato pickers are from and where some had accumulated experience from participation in these movements back home. A three-pronged strategy to counteract exploitation included:

1. Peer education of hired farm laborers;
2. Negotiations with major buyers/companies to pay more per pound and return the bonus to worker paychecks, and building support through a national consumer network; and
3. Production and financial monitoring through a third party, the Fair Food Standards Council (Asbed 2007; see also Asbed and Sellers 2013).

CIW took their fight to fast food giants. In 2001, CIW launched the first-ever farmworker-led boycott of a major fast food company, Taco Bell. The fast food chain's owner, Yum! Brands, is the world's largest restaurant company whose holdings include KFC, Pizza Hut, Long John Silver, and A&W. Typical of today's global corporate behemoths, purchasing is centralized. Starting with a cross-country bus and van tour of rallies and protests, CIW got student activists involved in consumer education through a Student/Farmworker Alliance. The message was simple: We want the public to help value the dignity of every person/worker so they may live a life free of degradation. Four years later (in 2005), Taco Bell agreed to all CIW demands. The company signed a "Fair Food Agreement" with a human-rights based or Code of Conduct that calls for paying a penny a pound more for tomatoes and monitoring of farms and workplaces by an independent Fair Food Council. Taco Bell and other companies that comply can place the Fair Food Program logo on food for purchase. The (green) tomatillo-colored logo depicts a woman with a full basket of tomatoes on her right shoulder with the words: Fair Food. Consumer Powered. Worker Certified. (Industrial tomatoes are picked when they are green and firm, then gassed with ethylene to appear ripe or red.)[3]

McDonalds became the second company to sign on in 2007, followed by Burger King and Subway in 2008. Chipotle's slogan is "food with integrity." But when CIW challenged that (Alkon 2014), Chipotle signed in 2012. Today, coast to coast, at almost any fast food restaurant in the USA—with the notable exception of Wendy's—you are likely eating a fair food tomato. And tomato pickers are earning $60–$80 more per week.[4]

CIW then moved to the largest catering and food service providers, making agreements with Compass Group, Aramark, Sodexho, and Bon Appétit Management. These are suppliers of food services in colleges and universities, corporate and hospital cafeterias, as well as stadiums and ballparks. Supermarkets like Whole Foods (in 2008) and Trader Joe's (in 2012) also joined the Fair Food Program. In 2014, Walmart joined and pledged to expand the program beyond tomatoes and beyond Florida. This agreement is pivotal because Walmart sells 20% of all tomatoes sold in the USA. In July of 2015, Ahold USA became the first mainline grocery (Giant, Stop & Shop, and Peapod) to sign the Fair Food Agreement. Publix Supermarket, the largest employee-owned supermarket chain in the USA and one of the ten largest in the country, has been a holdout. Paying one penny more per pound would double worker wages and cost Publix $1 million per year, a tiny part of their $2 billion in annual profits. On the consumer side, a family of four would see their grocery bill go up 44 cents per year for tomatoes.

Like the fair trade movement, CIW worked with student activists on college campuses and threatened boycotts of food outlets that would not negotiate with them. This is one reason for their success, according to Hesterman (2011, 64). The tactics are similar to the consumer boycotts led by Cesar Chavez to win initial union recognition for the United Farm Workers in the 1960s and 1970s. The CIW model, though, interrogates the entire food supply chain. If Trader Joe's pays a living wage to its retail employees, that is a good thing. But this strategy holds them accountable for paying living wages throughout their supply chain.

The Fair Food Program now covers about 90% of the Florida tomato industry. The extent of coverage is excellent because in the fields and (without the logo) in packaging, it is virtually impossible to distinguish the tomatoes to be shipped to chains who signed the Fair Food Agreement from those that did not. But assurances about what is and is not a fair food tomato improved when the Florida Tomato Growers Exchange joined the Fair Food Program in 2010, as they agreed to outside monitoring to assure that its tomatoes would meet the fair food standards.

Tomatoes are just the tip of the iceberg (pun intended). It is important to provide living wages for workers who pick lettuce in the south, then head to New Jersey or Maine to pick blueberries in the spring, and on to New York to pick apples in the fall. Food production is a huge industry. Just over 1 million hired farmworkers in the USA are responsible for helping to feed 325 million people in 125 million households, that is, 1 worker for every 325 people. The majority are employed by the largest farms, that is, those with sales over $500,000 per year. About 56% work in crops and 44% in livestock. The two largest states—California and Texas—account for more than a third of these workers

(U.S. Department of Agriculture 2016). In today's political economy, strategies must address human rights and worker rights throughout global supply chains.[5] It makes organizing more challenging, but the Coalition of Immokalee Workers demonstrates the possibility of progressive institutional change. Moving beyond tomatoes, CIW is now working on behalf of Florida bell pepper pickers and the entire produce industry.

Some Lessons for Institutional Change

The Immokalee workers' story provides two lessons for institutional change. The first lesson has to do with the power of retailers in global supply chains. Retail food distribution—comprised of grocery stores, mass merchandisers, drug stores, convenience stores and other food service facilities—totaled over $5 trillion in 2014, which constitutes about 28% of US GDP. Oxfam has weighed in on global supply chains, calling for a living wage throughout the chain. Oxfam's "Behind the Brands" campaign has rated and ranked the top 10 global food and drink companies on their supply chain policies against a transparent scorecard—living wages but also women's rights and other concerns. Oxfam denotes a spectrum (illegal road, low road, medium road, and high road) and provides examples of companies that are role models in particular areas (Oxfam 2014).

The second lesson is that labor unions are not the only effective institutional structure for worker organizing. Worker centers operating in coalition with others provide another model. CIW has spawned successors (see Greenhouse 2015; Miller 2015). One is the Retail Action Project in New York City, which we covered in Chap. 4 on the gig economy. Another is Somos Un Pueblo Unido, an advocacy group for immigrant workers in Santa Fe, New Mexico; it is helping workers in car washes and restaurants demand decent working conditions. The Restaurant Opportunities Center United (ROC) is working to increase the pay and improve working conditions among food workers in the food service industry (e.g., kitchen workers and servers). ROC United and its restaurant cooperative are considered in the next chapter on doing business responsibly.

Notes

1. *Food Chains* won the DOC IMPACT AWARD from the BritDoc Foundation in 2016, an award for documentary films that have had the greatest impact on society.

2. Those interested in other features of the "fair food movement"—from growing to production to consumption—may want to read the book, *Fair Food*, by agronomist and Fair Food Network funder Oran Hesterman (2011) or *Buying into Fair Trade* by Keith Brown (2013).
3. Some consumers may remember the 1978 Buy American, "Look for the Union Label" television advertising campaign by the International Ladies' Garment Workers Union, which included a short song. Labeling products to encourage consumers to consider working conditions when making purchases dates back to Progressive Era activism by the National Consumers' League and garment workers unions.
4. As of 2016, Wendy's still refuses to join the Fair Food Program. Journalists have uncovered that the chain purchases some of its fresh tomatoes from Mexico instead. A list of program adopters is contained in the 2015 annual report on the CIW website. See also Fair Foods Standards Council (2014).
5. When a global supply chain is committed to a set of principles to improve worker well-being, such as living wages or fair trade, it can be termed a values-based supply chain.

Supplementary Applications

1. The *Food Chains* documentary can be downloaded from iTunes. After viewing the film, summarize some of the strategies used in the film. Why do you think they were successful?
2. Conduct some research on the progress toward achieving a living wage for other fair food fruits and vegetables.
3. Go to the website called Behind the Brands at www.behindthebrands.org, which is part of Oxfam America. Behind the Brands rates the ten largest food brands on a range of issues from the treatment of workers to environmental policies. Click on the scorecard to understand how it is constructed. Then click on brands, select a brand that you consume, and see how it rates on various criteria.

References

Alkon, Alison Hope. 2014. Food Justice and the Challenge to Neoliberalism. *Gastronomica: The Journal of Critical Food Studies* 14 (2): 27–40.

Asbed, Greg. 2007. Coalition of Immokalee Workers: '!Golpear a Uno Es Golpear a Todos!' To Beat One of Us Is to Beat Us All. In *Bringing*

Human Rights Home, ed. Cynthia Soohoo, Catherine Albisa, and Martha F. Davis, vol. 3, 1–23. *Portraits of the Movement*. Santa Barbara, CA: Praeger Publishers.

Asbed, Greg, and Sean Sellers. 2013. The Fair Food Program: Comprehensive, Verifiable and Sustainable Change for Farmworkers. *University of Pennsylvania Journal of Law and Social Change* 16 (1): 39–48.

Bales, Kevin, and Ron Soodalter. 2010. *The Slave Next Door: Human Trafficking and Slavery in America Today*. Berkeley, CA: University of California Press.

Brown, Keith R. 2013. *Buying Into Fair Trade: Culture, Morality, and Consumption*. New York: New York University Press.

Caldwell, Katherine L. 2011. With Great Power Comes Responsibility: Grassroots Corporate Campaigns for Workers' Human Rights. *Journal of Poverty Law and Policy* 45 (5–6): 225–232.

Estabrook, Barry. 2009. Politics of the Plate: The Price of Tomatoes. *Gourmet*, March. http://www.gourmet.com/magazine/2000s/2009/03/politics-of-the-plate-the-price-of-tomatoes.html.

Estabrook, Barry. 2012. *Tomatoland: How Modern Industrial Agriculture Destroyed Our Most Alluring Fruit*. Kansas City, MO: Andrews McMeel Publishing.

Fair Food Standards Council (FFSC). 2014. *Annual Report*. www.fairfoodstandards.org.

Food Chains [Video]. 2014. http://www.foodchainsfilm.com/.

Gray, Margaret. 2014. *Labor and the Locovore: The Making of a Comprehensive Food Ethic*. Berkeley: University of California Press.

Greenhouse, Steven. 2015. Workers Organize, but Don't Unionize, to Get Protection Under Labor Law. *New York Times*, September 7, B1, B5.

Hesterman, Oran B. 2011. *Fair Food: Growing a Healthy, Sustainable Food System for All*. New York: Public Affairs.

Miller, Justin. 2015. Workers Centers: Organizing the 'Unorganizable'. *The American Prospect*, 26 February 2015. http://prospect.org/article/workers-centers-organizing-unorganizable.

Oxfam International. 2014. *Steps Towards a Living Wage in Global Supply Chains*, Oxfam Issue Briefing, December 2014, Oxford. https://www.oxfam.org/en/research/steps-towards-living-wage-global-supply-chains.

U.S. Department of Agriculture. 2016. *Farm Labor: Background*. Washington, DC: U.S. Department of Agriculture, Economic Research Service. http://www.ers.usda.gov/topics/farm-economy/farm-labor/background.aspx.

CHAPTER 6

Doing Business Responsibly: ROC United and Restaurant Workers

Abstract Colors Restaurant & Bar in New York City has made a name for itself by serving as a role model for the equitable treatment of workers in the traditionally low-paid restaurant industry. As described in this chapter, this cooperative enterprise also illustrates that businesses can operate with multiple motivations beyond profit maximization. Colors Restaurant is an unanticipated byproduct of Restaurant Opportunities Centers-United (ROC-U), a membership organization initially formed by restaurant workers displaced from jobs in the World Trade Center after 9/11. ROC-U operates Colors as part-restaurant, part-training facility, and part-exemplar of "high road" employment practices. ROC-U's other campaigns (such as "One Fair Wage") and litigation have secured pledges for better wages and working conditions from some larger restaurant conglomerates in the United States.

Keywords Cooperatives · Labor rights · Socially responsible business Ethical consumption

JEL Codes J31 · J54 · J61 · J81 · L31 · L66 · P13

One of the first things I noticed when I walked into the Colors Restaurant & Bar[1] in lower Manhattan (New York City) on May 28, 2015, was a chalkboard with a quote attributed to the late Cesar Chavez, co-founder with Delores Huerta of the United Farm Workers union. It read: "In the final analysis, it really doesn't matter what the political system is... We don't need perfect political systems; we need perfect participation." The décor also includes pictures from US labor movement history and contemporary restaurant worker protests. Colors has made a name for itself by serving as a role model for the equitable treatment of workers in the traditionally low-paid restaurant industry. It also illustrates that businesses can operate with multiple motivations beyond profit maximization. We need to recognize the range of business models that are possible in our economy and promote those that treat workers fairly.

Colors Restaurant & Bar is an unanticipated byproduct of Restaurant Opportunities Centers United (ROC-U), a membership organization to support restaurant workers. Colors operates as a *cooperative* enterprise, where its members are owners, and any surplus earnings are distributed among the members. ROC-U operates Colors as part-restaurant, part-training facility, and part-exemplar of high road employment practices.

According to the U.S. Small Business Administration (SBA), forming a cooperative is different from forming any other business entity. To start a cooperative, potential members (workers, consumers, or some other group) must agree on a common need and create a strategy on how to meet that need. Cooperative businesses in the USA operate in a diverse range of industries including food suppliers (food coops), banking (credit unions), personal services (child care centers), real estate (housing coops), utilities (local electric, fuel, and internet service providers), and even large companies such as Recreational Equipment, Inc. (REI) and Land O'Lakes dairies. About 40,000 different cooperatives conduct business in the USA, as per the 2015 annual report of the National Cooperative Business Association, CLUSA International (NCBA CLUSA 2015). As a form of business, cooperatives may or may not be incorporated. They operate to advance the interests of their members, and the interests may not be limited to profits (Birchall 2012). The members of Colors, for example, own and operate the restaurant in order to further social movement goals.

When Colors opened in 2006, it sought to promote a "high road" to restaurant profitability. Workers earned a starting wage of at least $14.50 per hour (though it was later lowered to about $9.00 per hour). They were covered by health insurance, they received paid time off, and they were assured potential promotions from within. As of 2016, the restaurant still operated with a slight loss on its accounting spreadsheets.

But it opts to do business differently. Management knows that it could likely generate positive profits if it were open for lunch as well as dinner. Yet it prefers to use those daytime hours to offer free training and professional development for industry workers. Fighting for living wages and better working conditions for restaurant workers is integral to their business model.

Turning a Tragedy into a Movement

The September 11, 2001, terrorist attacks on the World Trade Center in New York City played a role in the eventual establishment of Colors Restaurant. On the 107th floor atop World Trade Center Tower One (north tower) sat Windows on the World, an exclusive restaurant with panoramic views of the skylines of New York and New Jersey. It employed over 300 workers, 73 of whom lost their lives on that fateful day. The workers were a close-knit community, with many immigrants hailing from all corners of the globe.

One surviving worker of Moroccan descent was Fekkak Mamdouh. Through his union, Local 100 of the Hotel and Restaurant Employees Union (HERE), he volunteered his services in the aftermath of September 11. His own experience as a struggling restaurant employee was echoed in the experiences of those he was helping. As Rinku Sen writes, with Mamdouh, of his reflections at the time: "For the immigrants in Mamdouh's community, their ongoing experience of hardship in turn helped them to see the systemic nature of their problems, which would ultimately help them create a counter-memory" (2008, 43).

In October 2001, only 1 month later, union officials approached Fekkak Mamdouh about formalizing a long-term organization to help restaurant workers improve their wages and working conditions. HERE introduced Mamdouh to Saru Jayaraman, an attorney, organizer, activist, and first-generation Indian-American. They began working together and in early 2002 had a name for their new group: the Restaurant Opportunities Center of New York, or ROC-NY. The group included a number of former Windows on the World Employees.[2] When Jayaraman began to talk to Mamdouh about organizing restaurant workers, he replied: "But how can you organize people who can't even pay their own rent?" She answered, "That's the best time to organize, when people have nothing to lose" (quoted in Sen and Mamdouh 2008, 72).

ROC was forced to switch into a high gear almost immediately because of an informational picket line and a published phone number. In June of 2002, the former owner of Windows on the World Restaurant opened a new restaurant in midtown Manhattan. But he only hired back a few of his surviving 9/11 employees. ROC organized a picket of the new restaurant (Noché), alerting the media. Fekkak Mamdouh led the chanting. A New York City cable news channel covering the action put the ROC telephone number on the television screen; then the phone starting ringing and ringing, and ROC grew exponentially. The organization has since helped individual workers challenge managers over claims of stolen tips and wages, sexual harassment, and discrimination. The time-consuming service work was accomplished by confronting restaurants one at a time, employer by employer, on behalf of workers.[3]

By 2008, ROC became a national organization, changing its name to ROC United. Initially, the work continued to be very service oriented, one-on-one. Soon, however, ROC-U began to publish notable reports about the state of the restaurant industry's workers. It now has ongoing campaigns for higher tipped minimum wage laws, higher state and federal minimum wages, better health standards, greater upward mobility in employment, and guaranteed mandatory sick days. ROC-U—along with the Retail Action Project, Jobs with Justice, StudentLoanJustice.org, OUR Walmart, the Coalition of Immokalee Workers, and Fast Food Forward—is an example of the "alt-labor" response to the neoliberal economy. Rather than collective bargaining, alt-labor advocacy groups focus on community-based organizing around employment and economic policy issues in response to mounting income inequality.

The restaurant industry is one of the largest sectors in the US economy; it currently employs over 11.5 million workers and is projected to grow larger by 2020, according to the Bureau of Labor Statistics (BLS 2017). Restaurant work is a significant employment option for working mothers (ROC-U 2013). Yet, in her book *Behind the Kitchen Door* (2013), Jayaraman calls the industry "the absolutely lowest-paying employer in the United States" (quoted in Jobin-Leeds and AgitArte 2016, 120). Restaurants have seven of the ten lowest paying jobs in the USA. Jobs tend to be segregated along racial–ethnic lines, with people of color shunted to lower paid "back-of-the-house" work in the kitchen where they toil as a line cook, food preparer, or dishwasher.[4] Restaurant workers lack adequate wages, sick days, health insurance, and other benefits. Further, they often have erratic and unpredictable work schedules, just like the retail employees profiled in Chap. 4. Unregulated work off-the-clock (coming in early to prep and/or staying late) is prevalent; this is considered "wage theft." Wage theft also occurs when management under-reports worker tips on a paycheck or does not "top up" a lower tipped wage to the required state or federal minimum wage, as required by law (see DeFilippis et al. 2009).

Restaurant workers are in a relatively weak position to make their case. Fewer than 3% of New York City restaurant workers, for example, belong to labor unions. The powerful influence of the employers' lobby, National Restaurant Association (NRA), often dwarfs unions such as Hotel and Restaurant Employees (HERE, now merged with another union as UNITE-HERE) in the halls of Congress. The NRA has helped keep the national minimum wage for a worker who receives tips at $2.13 per hour since 1991. An average restaurant server at a casual eatery, even with tips, rarely earns more than the federal minimum wage of $7.35 per hour. ROC-U studies, in fact, indicate that only 20% of restaurant jobs pay a living wage of $13.47 or higher. And nine out of ten workers do not get employer-sponsored health insurance. Workers regularly complain of verbal abuse and harassment because of their immigration status, race, gender, or language skills.[5]

Saru Jayaraman's academic credentials (Yale Law School alumna and former director of the Food Labor Research Center at the University of California-Berkeley) and high-quality research seem to be matched only by her energy and organizing skills. She has envisioned and shaped ROC's campaigns, including protests and litigation against employers. Upon interviewing her, a *New York Times* reporter aptly declared: "For the Kitchen Help, She Stands the Heat" (Richardson 2005). ROC-U reports it has prevailed in fifteen specific campaigns against restaurant companies, winning more than $10 million for workers in cases involving back wages, sexual harassment, and stolen tips and wages. When customers are dining out, it is bad public relations to see workers are outside holding signs that read "Hungry for Justice." Winning over employers through education, moral suasion, or legal action, ROC-U has secured pledges for better wages and working conditions.

ROC-U has particularly targeted popular, high-profile, fine dining restaurants rather than small, family-owned restaurants. Fine dining sets standards for the industry that can then be followed by casual dining and fast-food restaurants (Brady 2014, 234). Large restaurant conglomerates, like the Darden Restaurant Group, Fireman Hospitality Group,

Smith & Wollensky Restaurant Group, are another target. Darden—the world's largest casual dining company—owns Red Lobster, Olive Garden, LongHorn Steakhouse, Capital Grille Steakhouse, and other national chains. After the passage of the Affordable Care Act (ACA or Obamacare), Darden announced it would limit worker hours to avoid paying for health care under the ACA. But ROC organized protests and urged consumer boycotts. Profits subsequently fell. And Darden reversed its decision.[6]

ROC-U also tries to affect public policy. An example is the "One Fair Wage" campaign. "It's time to do more than raise the tipped minimum wage" is the opening line introducing the campaign on the ROC website. ROC is working city by city and state by state to secure a decent minimum wage for all restaurant employees, not the lower tipped wage, often termed a sub-minimum wage. The tide is turning. More US states now require employers to pay workers more than the federal tipped minimum wage, under which some workers earn as little as $2.13 per hour (U.S. Department of Labor, Wage and Hour Division 2016). ROC collaborates with renowned chefs to try to eliminate the practice of tipping altogether and instead raising prices a little to thereby raise wages across the board; notable celebrity chefs such as Tom Colicchio (of Craft Restaurants) and Danny Meyer (Union Square Hospitality Group and founder of Shake Shack) have moved to eliminate tipping in their restaurants (Jayaraman 2016, 72–77).

Perhaps ROC's most ambitious project to date is the *Diner's Guide to Ethical Eating*. As discussed in Jayaraman's book, *Forked: A New Standard for American Dining* (2016), the guide was created in 2007 for New York City restaurants and in 2012 became a national smartphone app. "High road" restaurants are differentiated from "low road" based on four major factors: (1) Is a $10 or more wage paid to non-tipped workers? (2) Does the hourly wage for tipped workers exceed the minimum? (3) Are paid sick days provided? and (4) To what extent does the restaurant award raises and internal promotions? The guide is intended as a seal of approval akin to the popular Zagat's ratings.

It Is About More Than the Food

On opening day in 2006, the staff of Colors represented 22 countries; a global menu was based on family recipes. The name Colors is meant to pay living tribute to the ethnic mélange of the former Windows on the World workers. It took hard work, large donations, and in-kind labor to get it off the ground. The first several years were challenging, to say the least. There are tensions in any new business. A new cooperative has to work out relationships between organizers and workers while trying to keep itself afloat.

Colors offers locally sourced ingredients that are not genetically modified. In 2014, it launched its 100% gluten-free menu. Other restaurants, of course, have joined the locavore trend. What sets Colors apart is *how* it does business, its ownership, management, and labor relations policies. All workers are paid a living wage. Front-of-the-house workers are paid the state minimum wage plus tips, which are pooled and shared. Workers have health insurance, paid time off, and a pension. All non-management employees are union members. Colors is a member of RAISE (Restaurants Advancing Industry Standards in Employment), a national association of over 100 restaurants with high road business practices advocating on behalf of all restaurant workers. The restaurant is run by a general manager, with an executive chef and a wine director. These professionals have their roles, but consistent with a business goal of empowering workers and improving worker well-being, they act as teammates more than traditional bosses.

Most employees in the restaurant industry have not attended—nor could they afford to attend—a culinary training institute. Thousands of restaurant workers have walked through the doors of Colors to take advantage of free training opportunities. The CHOW Institute (Colors Hospitality & Opportunities for Workers) offers professional development classes to restaurant workers seeking advancement within the industry. Part-time hospitality training courses typically last 8 weeks; occasional seminars are also provided. To enable workers to move into better jobs in high-end restaurants, topics have included how to set tables, how to serve tables, and how to taste and pour wine.

The Colors model is expanding. Colors restaurants have opened in Detroit, Michigan (in 2012), New Orleans, Louisiana (2016), Washington, DC (2016), and East Oakland, California (2016). These businesses send a message with every meal they serve: "ROC is not trying to prove, with COLORS or its High Road work or anything else, that it is easy to run an ethical restaurant; a place that serves not just sustainably-sourced food but which promotes a sustainable career path for servers, cooks, runners, bussers, and the millions of people that serve food to diners across the United States. It's trying to prove that it's a worthwhile endeavor" (Ralph 2015).

Changing How Business Gets Done

You do not need to be a cooperative like Colors Restaurant to have equitable treatment of workers. ROC-U currently counts 80,000 restaurant workers, 200 high-road employers, their members, and thousands of customers as part of their national movement. Their power comes from the combined efforts of worker organizing, socially conscious consumers, and an alternative vision of what business entails. Profit maximization is not a legal requirement for businesses, nor is it a financial necessity to minimize costs; firms and entrepreneurs, like individuals, may, therefore, have multiple motivations for operating their businesses (Nelson 2006; Warnecke 2014). Claims to the contrary are made by those who imagine a mythical economy where cutthroat competition requires firms to operate at peak efficiency. Institutional economists prefer to study how economies actually function. Once we acknowledge that real markets consistently deviate from perfectly competitive models, the door is open to progressive institutional change in our conception of business.

ROC-U brings together two alternative business models: cooperatives (member-owned businesses) and social entrepreneurship. Alternative ownership strategies such as cooperatives are part of what Gar Alperovitz (2006) describes as a *progressive ownership society*. In such a society, shared ownership gives people a stake in their community and forges interpersonal bonds, contributing to sustainable economic development. Democratized forms of ownership provide a more viable long-term strategy for progressive change, according to advocates, than liberal reforms based on state intervention (Alperovitz 2011). Or, as economist Nancy Folbre writes, "By demonstrating the viability of businesses aimed to serve larger social goals, cooperatives have altered our economic ecology" (2013, 26). Social entrepreneurship is a term that has emerged for businesses where "[s]ocial good or benefit, not shareholder profit, is the mission focus" (Stecker 2014, 352). Originally associated with developing countries, social entrepreneurship has emerged as a new institutional form situated on a spectrum between non-profits and traditional business firms. Even when such firms are individually owned, they are structured to emphasize social sustainability (Warnecke 2014).[7]

Consumption is also more complex than the standard treatment in neoclassical economic theory. The act of consumption is a social process. It sends messages. It also expresses and constructs identity: "The practice of buying, cooking, and eating food is a feature of everyday life that reproduces bodies and identities" (Pietrykowski 2004, 310; see also Todorova 2014). Like many (though not all) of its customers, I chose to dine at Colors as an ethically conscious consumer, an act of political consumerism or "buycotting" (the opposite of boycotting). Since then, I have tried other restaurants listed in the Diners' Guide to Ethical Eating app on my iPhone. Conscious consumption, like social entrepreneurship, embraces goals beyond those of the individual. Knowing that the employees are treated equitably and that my funds were furthering the work of ROC-U mattered. Besides, as a follower of a gluten-free diet for medical reasons, I ate the best fried chicken I have ever had, gluten-free or not.

Notes

1. Legally, the name is in all capital letters: COLORS.
2. The history and activities of Colors and ROC have been covered periodically in the press, even the pages of prominent *Forbes* magazine, e.g., Lawrence (2006), Eichler (2011), Ralph (2015), and Gelles (2016). My story is partially drawn from those sources, but primarily from Saru Jayaraman's two books (2013, 2016), Rinku Sen's book with Fekkak Mamdouh (2008), and the ROC-U website.
3. ROC's early days are described in Chap. 4 of Sen with Mamdouh (2008) and Brady (2014).
4. Such occupational segregation was also uncovered at dining facilities and restaurants in the casino industry, according to Mutari and Figart (2015).
5. These studies may be found at http://rocunited.org/our-work/research-policy/.
6. ROC also secured a settlement with Fireman's Hospitality Group, owner of the Redeye Grill (near Carnegie Hall) and Café Fiorello (near Lincoln Center) (see Brady 2014).
7. Social entrepreneurship is distinct from "Corporate Social Responsibility" (CSR), the idea that firms may engage in voluntary actions to promote a public purpose so long as this contributes to or at least does not interfere with profitability (see Yunus 2007). For an excellent introduction to CSR, see Crane et al. (2013).

Supplementary Applications

1. What national chain restaurants do you like to visit for a meal with friends or family? Do you know how they treat their lowest paid workers? Go to the ROC-United website and download (for Android or iPhone) the *Diner's Guide to Ethical Eating*. This free app provides employment information on the most popular restaurants in America in major cities across the country, from Los Angeles to Washington, DC to New York City. Select all the "high-road" options for wages and working conditions and select a city near you to see a list of restaurants. Click on specifics. Try eating at a high road and a low road restaurant, if possible. Notice any differences? If a restaurant you are visiting is not listed in the app, you can add it to the database if you have the employment information.

References

Alperovitz, Gar. 2006. The Wealth of Neighborhoods. *Democracy: A Journal of Ideas*, 19–32. http://democracyjournal.org/magazine/1/the-wealth-of-neighborhoods/.

Alperovitz, Gar. 2011. The Emerging Paradoxical Possibility of a Democratic Economy. *Review of Social Economy* 60 (3): 377–391.

Birchall, Johnston. 2012. The Comparative Advantages of Member-owned Businesses. *Review of Social Economy* 70 (3): 263–294.

Brady, Marnie. 2014. An Appetite for Justice: The Restaurant Opportunities Center of New York. In *New Labor in New York: Precarious Workers and the Future of the Labor Movement*, ed. Ruth Milkman and Ed Ott, 229–245. Ithaca, NY: Cornell University Press/ILR Press.

Crane, Andrew, Dirk Matten, and Laura J. Spence. 2013. *Corporate Social Responsibility: Readings and Cases in Global Context*, 2nd ed. London: Routledge.

DeFilippis, James, Nina Martin, Annette Bernhardt, and Siobhán McGrath. 2009. On the Character and Organization of Unregulated Work in the Cities of the United States. *Urban Geography* 30 (1): 63–90.

Eichler, Alexander. 2011. Former Windows on the World Employees Become Advocates for Fair Treatment of Service Workers. http://www.huffingtonpost.com/2011/09/09/windows-on-the-world-fair-treatment-of-workers_n_951026.html.

Folbre, Nancy. 2013. Co-op Economics. *Dollars & Sense*, September/October: 25–29.

Gelles, David. 2016. An Outspoken Force to Give Food Workers a Seat at the Table. *New York Times*, February 20.
Jayaraman, Saru. 2013. *Behind the Kitchen Door*. Ithaca, NY: Cornell University Press.
Jayaraman, Saru. 2016. *Forked: A New Standard for American Dining*. New York: Oxford University Press.
Jobin-Leeds, Greg, and AgitArte. 2016. *When We Fight We Win!* New York: The New Press.
Lawrence, John. 2006. COLORS Restaurant. *Dollars & Sense*, July/August.
Mutari, Ellen, and Deborah M. Figart. 2015. *Just One More Hand: Life in the Casino Economy*. Lanham, MD: Rowman & Littlefield.
National Cooperative Business Association, CLUSA International (NCBA CLUSA). *Cooperatives Build A Better World: 2015 Annual Report*. Washington, DC: NCBA CLUSA. http://www.ncba.coop/.
Nelson, Julie A. 2006. *Economics for Humans*. Chicago: University of Chicago Press.
Pietrykowski, Bruce. 2004. You Are What You Eat: The Social Economy of the Slow Food Movement. *Review of Social Economy* 62 (3): 307–321.
Richardson, Lynda. 2005. For the Kitchen Help, She Stands the Heat. *New York Times*, January 21.
Ralph, Talia. 2015. The Non-Profit Restaurant That Could. *Forbes*, October 6.
ROC (Restaurant Opportunities Centers) United. 2013. *The Third Shift: Child Care Needs and Access for Working Mothers in Restaurants*. New York: ROC United. http://rocunited.org/the-third-shift/.
Sen, Rinku, and Fekkak Mamdouh. 2008. *The Accidental American: Immigration and Citizenship in the Age of Globalization*. San Francisco: Berrett-Koehler Publishers.
Stecker, Michelle J. 2014. Revolutionizing the Nonprofit Sector through Social Entrepreneurship. *Journal of Economic Issues* 48 (2): 349–358.
Todorova, Zdravka. 2014. Consumption as a Social Process. *Journal of Economic Issues* 48 (3): 663–678.
U.S. Department of Labor, Bureau of Labor Statistics (BLS). 2017. Industries at a Glance: Food Services and Drinking Places. http://www.bls.gov/iag/tgs/iag722.htm.
U.S. Department of Labor, Wage and Hour Division. 2016. Minimum Wages for Tipped Employees. August 1, 2016. https://www.dol.gov/whd/state/tipped.htm.
Warnecke, Tonia L. 2014. The 'Individualist Entrepreneur' vs. Socially Sustainable Development: Can Microfinance Build Community? *Journal of Economic Issues* 48 (2): 377–386.
Yunus, Muhammad. 2007. *Creating a World Without Poverty: Social Business and the Future of Capitalism*. New York: Public Affairs.

CHAPTER 7

Swimming in Debt: Student Loans and the Fight to Save a Generation

Abstract In 2010, student loan debt surpassed credit card debt for the first time in US history. Default rates have increased following the Great Recession. Yet student debt, unlike most debt, is not dischargeable in bankruptcy, leaving those burdened by loans unable to move on with their lives. Hundreds of alumni from the private, for-profit Corinthian Colleges Inc. have proclaimed a debt strike, refusing to pay off their student loans. They assert they were defrauded by aggressive recruitment and specious promises about jobs, while Corinthian profited from federal loan funds. The seeds of this debt resistance movement, sown in the wake of Occupy Wall Street, are growing. The activism described in this chapter raises questions about the provisioning and financing of higher education in the neoliberal era.

Keywords Student loans · Debt · Debt strike · Higher education

JEL Codes I22 · I23 · G28 · H4

In the USA television network series *Mr. Robot*, an anarchist recruits and heads up a group of computer hackers, called the fsociety. The "hactivists" seek to cancel all consumer debt by attacking the records of a large corporation called E Corp. In a 2000 animated short film from New Zealand director James Cunningham titled *Infection*, a digital engineered life form (or DELF) is deployed to infect a corporate computer system to destroy the student loan of its hacker-creator. Expunging student loan debt seems like the stuff of science fiction. Or is it?

Closer to reality, hundreds of alumni from the private, for-profit Corinthian Colleges Inc. have proclaimed a debt strike, refusing to pay off their student loans. The original fifteen created a debt collective dubbed the Corinthian Fifteen. They asserted they were defrauded by both aggressive recruitment and specious promises about jobs. The result was enormous profit for Corinthian and colossal debt loads for students. In February of 2015, the Corinthian Fifteen wrote a letter to the U.S. Department of Education making their case (see https://debtcollective.org/studentstrike). Their letter, which now serves as a model for the student debt strike movement opens with "We are not alone in this fight." It ends with "WE WON'T PAY. WE ARE THE CORINTHIAN FIFTEEN." The now over 200 Corinthian strikers and their supporters represent a larger movement for progressive institutional change in how we allocate the risks and rewards associated with student debt and higher education. The seeds of this debt resistance student movement were sown in the wake of the 2011 Occupy Wall Street movement.

In 2010, student loan debt surpassed credit card debt for the first time in US history. In 2013, outstanding student loan debt exceeded $1 trillion dollars. More than 40 million Americans had balances on student loans in 2014. That equates to one-in-five US households (Fry 2012). By 2016, student loan debt exceeded $1.3 trillion and is growing at the rate of $2700 a second according to MarketWatch.com's student loan debt clock. The Project on Student Debt (from the Institute for College Access & Success) reports that the average debt for an undergraduate from the Class of 2015 was $30,100, and the share of graduates with debt was 68%. It is not uncommon for the initial debt load at commencement to eventually double with fees tacked on for late payments and non-payment. Student debt is the only kind of household debt that continued to rise through and after the Great Recession. Default rates have grown, too, especially since the last recession; about 7 million Americans are in default on more than $100 billion in balances, according to the Consumer Finance Protection Bureau (CFPB).

The media often emphasizes the poor choices of individual debtors. Of course, the choice of college major and career still affects the level of affordable debt. Student borrowers need to be conscious of realistic job and salary prospects. A closer examination of the data, rather than individual anecdotes, reveals patterns that demonstrate the social and economic context that contributes to escalating default rates. Because of penalties, fees, and compound interest, lenders and loan servicers profit more from delinquent and defaulted loans than they do from loans in good standing. Student loans lack many of the basic consumer protections of other debt, like mortgages, credit card debt, auto loans, and outstanding tax obligations to the U.S. Internal Revenue Service. Can you refinance your student loan to get a lower interest rate like a mortgage loan? No. Can you rollover your student loans into one with a lower interest rate like a credit card? No. Can you have your student loans discharged in the case of personal bankruptcy like consumer debt, and even gambling debt? No. According to legal scholar Daniel Austin, "The student loan industry is a massive, profit-making enterprise. With loan assets of $1 trillion, and lending in 2013 exceeding $150 billion, the student loan business eclipses almost any private industry in annual sales" (2013, 338). It is a lucrative business. In 2013, government profits from student loans were surpassed only by the profits of Exxon and Apple (Shafer 2015, 127).

This chapter examines the evolution of institutions governing the provisioning and financing of higher education in the United States. Prior to the neoliberal era, this evolution exemplified progressive institutional change that reduced invidious class distinctions. The democratization of higher education was viewed as serving a public purpose by increasing economic productivity and contributing to citizen and community engagement. More recently, the tide has turned. In an increasingly financialized economy, public purpose has been replaced by socialized risk and privatized gains. Loans and their potentially profitable income streams are pooled and converted into financial instruments, at the same time that higher education is touted as a solution to stagnant middle class incomes in an era of inequality. Students who see this system as "rigged" in the favor of big financial players whose debts are bailed out by government wonder why they are expected to carry the burden of their debts.

THE DEMOCRATIZATION OF HIGHER EDUCATION

The democratization of access to higher education rested on a transformation of social norms about the purpose and funding of college. Centuries ago, higher education in the USA was primarily for the elite— the *leisure class* in Thorstein Veblen's terminology. An aristocratic family could afford to send their son to a private college or university (at least until the founding of selective women's colleges and normal schools to train schoolteachers). In other words, education was self-funded if you could earn admittance. US institutions, many with religious affiliations, copied the British model of a genteel education that reinforced class hierarchies. Knowledge of the classics and liberal arts, while often pursued for their intrinsic worth, were also status markers. In the late nineteenth century, higher education became a tool that served what economist John Kenneth Galbraith would later refer to as the *public purpose*. The Land-Grant College Act of 1862 upended the entire landscape of American higher education. Rather than simply socializing young gentlemen (and ladies), land-grant universities emphasized industrial and technical arts. They laid the ground for the public sector, state-supported colleges that later became the bedrock of American higher education.

Still, it was difficult for many in the emerging middle class to send their sons or daughters to college. Only after World War II could the new middle class reasonably consider higher education. A series of initiatives addressing affordability started with the Servicemen's Readjustment Act of 1944, better known as the "GI bill." The National Defense Higher Education Act of 1958 funded the first student loan program for higher education. The Higher Education Act (HEA) of 1965, instituted as part of President Lyndon B. Johnson's Great Society, created the Guaranteed Student Loan program (GSLs) (now called Stafford loans). Money would be lent by private-sector banks, but guaranteed by the federal government in case of default. To stimulate lending to students with no credit history, banks were paid a premium interest rate. Taking the process of democratization one step further, student loan programs during this era socialized the risks associated with paying for college. Yet private sector banks still reaped the rewards of repaid loans, the accumulated interest. Also included in the 1965 HEA were Pell grants for the neediest students.

Due to such policy initiatives, college and university attendance has grown over the decades. The number of borrowers subsequently swelled. The dollar value of new student loans issued increased tenfold from $1 billion in 1971 to $10 billion in 1986. It increased another 10 times to $100 billion by 2011 (Best and Best 2014). At first, the dollar trend was fueled by increased numbers of college students; the good news was that federal and university financial aid packages helped keep average debt per student borrower relatively low.

But in the 1990s, *average* debt loads began to skyrocket. Some comparisons illustrate the problem. Average debt load per borrower was approximately $9000 in 1993, $15,000 in 1999, and $20,000 in 2006 (from a chart by Izzo 2013). Average debt per borrower reached $28,950 for the Class of 2014. Thus, by my calculations, student debt per borrower increased 216% from 1993 to 2014 (in constant 2013 dollars). In contrast, the increase in the average price level in the US economy, as expressed by the CPI-U increased only 64% during the same period.

How Did We Get Here? Contributors to the Student Debt Crisis

Students, alumni, and parents in the neoliberal era are facing a restructuring of higher education that is reversing the process of democratization and returning to privatization of costs and risk. As part of this restructuring, a number of compounding factors have contributed to the emerging student loan crisis. First, American middle-class incomes (for parents who send their children to college and for young alumni who graduate) have stagnated since the 1990s. Families have been squeezed by deindustrialization, globalization, and deunionization. Income growth has basically been flat for the bottom 80% of US families since the start of the new millennium. College is viewed as a necessary response to these financial pressures, even as this new political economy landscape makes it harder for families to afford the rising costs.

But perhaps the lion's share of the explanation for the debt crisis is that federal and state governments have been decreasing their support for higher education. We have returned to a social norm of higher education as a relatively private good—an investment in one's individual human capital that must be emulated by those seeking class mobility. At the federal level, for example, funding for Pell grants has not kept pace with inflation. A reauthorization of the HEA in 1980 enabled parents to take out PLUS loans for their children's education; PLUS stands for Parent Loan for Undergraduate Students. Parents began taking on a new form of student debt during the period that they were accumulating consumer and mortgage debt. This form of debt is burdening an older generation that needs to be saving for retirement, in addition to the burdens experienced by student debtors. Changes at the state level

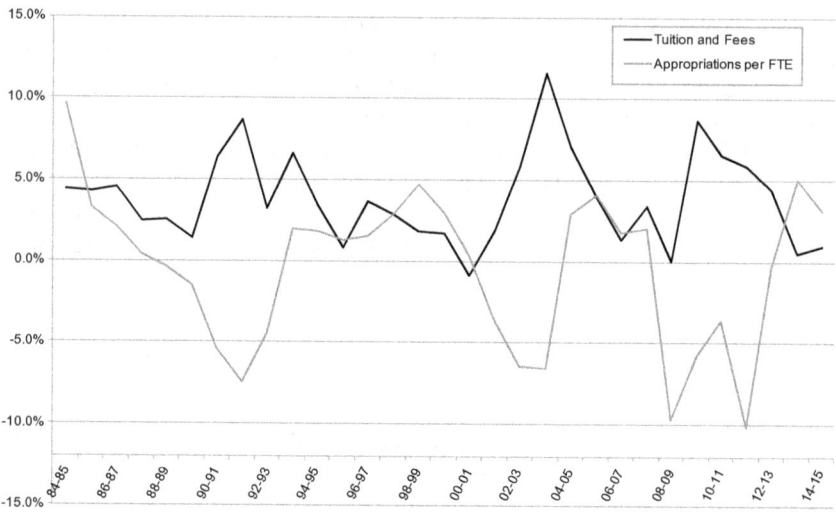

Fig. 7.1 Annual percentage change in inflation-adjusted per-student state funding for higher education and in tuition and fees at Public Institutions, 1984–1985 to 2014–2015

are even more critical. Almost three out of four US college and university students attend public institutions (as indicated by U.S. Department of Education annual enrollment statistics). Many stay within their home state. The percent attending public schools is also higher for non-whites than whites. Higher education spending is typically the third-largest category in state budgets (Pew 2015, Fig. 1), yet it has been subject to budget cutbacks just when the need is expanding. In fact, after the Great Recession, there was an uptick in enrollments in public institutions, as families sought to minimize costs.

For state institutions of higher education, tuition has increased as state support for higher education has fallen. Figure 7.1[1] portrays the rates of change in two indicators: annual percent changes in state support versus annual increases in tuition and fees. The figure spans 31 years, beginning with academic year 1984–1985 and ending with 2014–2015. The two trend lines resemble mirror images. The peaks of increases in tuition and fees correspond to the valleys of declines in state support. But as the rate of change in state support increases, the escalation in tuition and fees is lower, bringing the two lines closer together. The trend depicted in Fig. 7.1 has been pointed to over and over by state university presidents and some candidates for elected office. In a report titled *Higher Education: State Funding Trends and Policies on Affordability*, the U.S. Government Accountability Office has a similar graph (U.S. GAO 2014, Fig. 3). The GAO reports that median published tuition prices both at public 2-year and 4-year colleges increased by 55% from 2003 to 2012. To put it a different way, economists might say that the educational CPI has exceeded the overall CPI-U.

State disinvestment in higher education due to tight fiscal constraints, including less federal aid to state governments, has made public institutions more tuition dependent. Seeking to keep pace with technology, they have been investing in academic computing facilities, electronic classrooms, and digital subscriptions for libraries, and other state-of-the-art facilities. Some of these liabilities, such as subscriptions to library databases, were outside of their control. At the same time, colleges and universities are not blameless. Consumed by climbing up popular ranking systems such as the *U.S. News and World Report* annual survey, universities built well-equipped student housing and food courts, student centers with swimming pools, game arcades, and other markers of conspicuous consumption designed to attract students in a crowded market. Students were left holding the short straw—forced to fund the growing gap between state support and higher tuition and fees with debt.[2]

Once students graduate or leave school, the debt problem comes home to roost. Studies indicate that student loan debt has led young adults to postpone their marriages, delay saving for a mortgage and purchasing their first home, and shelve plans for starting retirement nest eggs. It can leave them without a car, unable to afford an auto loan. It negatively impacts their job selection. In professional practice areas such as law and medicine, it can affect their choice of specialty. Student loan debt has been found to hurt entrepreneurship and small business formation. More student debt is associated with a greater likelihood of declaring personal bankruptcy. In short, student loan debt reduces many aspects of well-being.[3]

Some students have been more at risk to bear these costs than others. In fact, the unequal distribution of student debt threatens to reinforce invidious distinctions, an ironic twist on the vision of higher education as a means of equalizing opportunity and providing a path for class mobility. Groups with higher debt levels include: African-American students (Jackson and Reynolds 2013; Goldrick-Rab and Kelchen

2015; Huelsman 2016; Baum 2016), Hispanic students (Ratcliffe and McKernan 2013), female students (Marez 2014), students from middle class households (Houle 2013), students who have declared themselves independent from their parent or parents (Baum 2015; Huelsman 2016), and students who are student parents themselves (Huelsman 2016). Not surprisingly, the highest average debtors are also students who attend *for-profit* colleges such as Corinthian and the University of Phoenix (Cellini and Darolia 2015). Unlike public institutions or non-profit colleges and universities, the mission of these business enterprises is primarily profit driven, and federal loans represent a desirable source of revenue.

Problems intensify for those who have trouble making payments due to job loss, reduced income, health crises, or divorce (see Carey 2015). Debtors who are late on their payments or miss payments can be victimized by aggressive loan servicing companies. The Consumer Finance Protection Bureau maintains a database of complaints (see CFPB 2015b). The majority of the complaints, about six in ten, focus on the abusive behavior of a loan service provider. The largest private loan company servicing these loans is the former Sallie Mae, now renamed Navient; it is also the servicer with the most complaints.[4]

Numerous studies demonstrate that the most at-risk for default are former students who do not complete their bachelor's degrees. Drop-outs are still responsible for repaying their student loan debt. "Incompleters," as borrowers who drop out are called, have higher unemployment rates. And they are more than four times likely to default than students who complete their education. So are students from for-profit institutions (see Nguyen 2012; Looney and Yannelis 2015). In fact, these two risk factors appear to be related. Lured by slick marketing, people who do not have the time and/or resources to become full-time students opt for the newer for-profit institutions, particularly online classes, then find themselves unable to keep up. Tuition is higher than for community colleges or 4-year public universities, although the programs are generally not accredited and the credits are not accepted by traditional colleges and universities if you transfer. Once students are enrolled, the for-profit institutions often do not have the equivalent support structures in place to help at-risk students complete their degrees (U.S. Senate Committee on Health, Education, Labor, and Pensions 2012). Rather than providing a learning community, the emphasis is on individual success and failure.

Student Debt Activism and Debt Forgiveness

Must one pay one's debts? The students and graduates who advocate debt strikes and jubilees (periods of debt forgiveness) are taking a controversial stand that seems to counter a deeply held belief—that a person who borrows money should pay what they owe. Debt is a legal contract, and legal contracts must be honored for our economic system to function. In reality, however, debts are not always paid. Contracts are breached, fraud can nullify them, and bankruptcy laws allow businesses and individuals to restructure and/or discharge their debts. In financial markets, debt is often bought and sold for a fraction of its original value. In fact, our current financial system is predicated on risk that obligations will not always be fulfilled. The cleansing of debt is a vital part of this system so that mistakes do not unduly haunt people.

Debts are problems for individuals. But en masse, debt becomes a structural problem. Some fear that student debt is emerging as the next financial bubble with a risk of systemic default—possibly as economically devastating as the bursting of the mortgage bubble in 2007. Paul Hampton has written: "Oil tycoon J. Paul Getty captured this succinctly when he said: 'If you owe the bank $100, that's your problem. If you owe the bank $100 million, that's the bank's problem'" (2015, 31). Or, in the mantra on the website of The Debt Collective (debtcollective.org), "Alone our debts are a burden; together they make us powerful." So how do debt activists propose to use their collective power? While some focus on the eradication or amelioration of existing debt, others seek solutions to the ongoing problem of how higher education can be accessible and affordable, in the hopes of forestalling another generation of debtors.

The radicalization of student debtors is an outgrowth of Occupy Wall Street, the ongoing movement that originated with protestors taking over Zuccotti Park in lower Manhattan in the fall of 2011. The occupation of Zuccotti Park, mere blocks away from Wall Street, lasted roughly 2 months. Occupy Wall Street became the symbolic center of a worldwide protest movement, embracing other concerns. Protestors were angry with the concentration of power and wealth in the increasingly financialized global economy and the impact of economic inequality on democratic political processes. While the physical manifestation of the Occupy movement faded as protesters were evicted from various locations, there were lasting effects in changing discourse and bringing attention to the economic hardship faced by the bottom "99 percent" who were not part of the elite. Out of these actions also sprang loosely connected networks of organizations and activists linked together via social media, memes, and a shared critique of concentrated economic power.

Although the larger movement wants to make changes to debt practices for all forms of debt, there has been a particular focus on student loan debt.[5] This makes sense both because of the youthful demographic involved in the Occupy movement as well as the relative rise of student loan debt compared with other forms of debt (like mortgages and credit cards). It is very difficult, though, to organize debtors for strategic resistance. Debtors owe money to different entities. With debt, unlike a labor union, there are no shared workplaces or physical sites for resistance. By targeting student loan debt, activists can pinpoint the top one or two student loan debt servicers, like Navient. Of course, the federal loans were really issued by the U.S. Department of Education, who in turn sold the debt to big banks, who repackaged it into securities bundles similar to the collateralized debt obligations that led to the financial crisis of 2008. So who, exactly, is the creditor? This has posed strategic challenges.

Consciousness raising, the hallmark of the women's liberation movement of the 1970s, has played an important role. For example, the Occupy Student Debt campaign created a website (that still exists) where student debtors could post and share stories about how much debt they had accumulated and how it has affected their lives. This site and others like it serve as places where, by sharing their individual experiences and recognizing themselves in others' stories, people realize that their problems are not the result of bad choices. Instead, they reveal the institutional context that framed their choices and limited their options.

One of the first organizations that emerged out of Occupy Student Debt in the summer of 2012 was Strike Debt (at debtstrike.org). Strike Debt started with 10 people and grew into a nationwide movement of debt resisters (Appel 2015a, 28). Their demands include free public education, student debt that is dischargeable in bankruptcy, and student loan forgiveness after a period of time such as 10 years. Their most innovative organizing model has been the concept of a *debt collective*, bringing debtors together to resist through debt strikes, as well as other forms of protest and advocacy. A Strike Debt collective would be akin to a union, a consumer's union. If need be, debtors could be organized around their loan servicer. At present, there are collectives for former Corinthian students and a Sallie Mae/Navient collective.

The organization initially launched a petition with the pledge that 1 million student debtors would sign, step forward, and refuse to pay their loans. But the organizers also understood that even if such a large debt strike withheld $27 billion from the system (1 million times average debt of $27,000), it would be a drop in the bucket nationally. Upon reflection, cofounder Pamela (Pam) Brown says they were naïve. This first campaign effort seemingly failed as Strike Debt fell far short of the target. Student loan debtors did not step forward to sign the Pledge of Refusal. Refusing to pay was scary. Also, most debtors did not question the morality of their debt. It was just the way life is. If they borrowed it, even if under unfair circumstances, they had to repay it. Still in its nascent stages, the Strike Debt organizers realized they needed to educate as well as organize.

A new idea arose: a "debt fairy." The fairy would wipe out student debt, but how? The organizers seized on an ancient idea, a jubilee. Jubilee is based on a concept of periodic debt forgiveness discussed in the Bible's Old Testament. Instead of a fixed period, however, Strike Debt launched the "Rolling Jubilee Fund" in the fall of 2012. The Rolling Jubilee used crowdfunding to buy defaulted debt on the secondary market and forgive it "as a political act of 'striking debt'" (Brown 2014, 1). Rolling Jubilee took the necessary steps to file all the regulatory paperwork to be certified as a debt collecting agency. Almost $32 million in debt from medical bills and student loans was erased, according to the ticker on the Rolling Jubilee website.

Although the fund has been dormant since 2013, Rolling Jubilee served as an important education tool, too. For example, only $700,000 was raised and used to purchase the debt that they forgave. The process demonstrated to debtors that the market value of what they owe can be as little as 2% of its original value, mere pennies on the dollar when default is assigned to collection. Yet even at a fraction of the cost, Pam Brown says that she knew that it would be impossible to crowdfund away debt. Instead, the action served as an important educational tool about the financial value of debt instruments and the morality of debt. It interrogates our understanding and acceptance of debt. In anthropologist and Occupy Wall Street raconteur Hannah Appel's eloquent words:

Thus Rolling Jubilee also encourages debtors to question the sanctity of the contract. Following debt's rhizomic paths, the project begins to pry open the creditor/debtor dyad, showing debts' proliferative form that to date, only creditors have been able to exploit. Again, as a tactic for building collective power this project is limited, but insofar as it begins to destabilize the sedimented moralities around consumer debt—that contracts are sacred, that everyone is equally obligated to pay their debts—it begins to erode some of the enduring realisms of the money form. (2015b, 430)

In simpler terms, a 2014 pamphlet by Strike Debt titled *The Debt Resisters' Operations Manual*, argued "We are under no moral obligation to keep our promises to liars and thieves. In fact, we are morally obligated to find a way to stop this system rather than continuing to perpetuate it."

Meanwhile, the debt collective movement has gained strength. They launched a day of action at college campuses in the USA, "1T day" on April 25, 2013, to signify when outstanding student loan debt in America would top the $1 trillion mark. The Corinthian Strike Debt project (that opened this chapter) has grown into a quasi-debtors union, Debt Collective. The Corinthian Collective now numbers at least 200 student borrowers, and they are supported by over 1200 "student solidarity strikers" from other colleges and universities who signed a pledge to refuse to pay their federal loans as well. Their activities have been covered in the media, and the Corinthian debt strike was even mentioned on a 2015 episode of the CBS television drama *The Good Wife*. The Debt Collective is taking on issues such as "teach-outs," which occur when for-profit colleges (including 17 branches of the "Art Institute" across the country) shut their doors. Teach-outs improvise ways of completing educational programs, but prevent students from having their debt discharged, which is usually an option if a school goes under.

Other organizations have taken up the fight, linking the student debt crisis to protests about rising tuition. For example, Jobs With Justice (JwJ), a coalition of community organizations, labor unions, and faith leaders, has teamed with the United States Student Association (USSA), the largest student-led organization in the USA. Together they formed the Student Labor Action Project (SLAP at studentlabor.org). SLAP organized the Million Student March on Thursday, November 12, 2015 (Twitter hashtag #MillionStudentMarch). At 110 campuses across the USA, students walked out of class to support free tuition at public colleges and universities, cancellation of all student debt, as well as a $15 minimum wage for all campus workers.

Debt strikes and jubilees have not been broad enough to impact large numbers of students and former students. (Of course, a new period of militancy could yet emerge that would engender more participation in these actions.) But, the student debtors' activism has succeeded in raising awareness, and their militancy motivated policy makers in the Obama administration to address the worst of the abuses.[6] Debt Collective, for example, is keeping the pressure on federal regulators, and they, in turn, are pressuring the for-profit institutions. The CFPB has filed lawsuits against several large offenders for predatory lending, asserting that students are rushed through the applications for federal and private loans, despite knowing that they were likely to default. The first big lawsuit was filed against Corinthian in September of 2014. On February 3, 2015, the CFPB announced student loan forgiveness of more than $480 million for borrowers of Corinthian College's high-cost private student loans. According to CFPB Director Richard Cordray, "These consumers were lured into high-cost loans destined to default [with advertised spurious job prospects and career services], and then targeted with aggressive debt ccollection tactics" (CFPB 2015a). The lawsuit nevertheless proceeded to the federal courts, and a $530 million judgment against Corinthian was awarded in October 2015. The regulators have ongoing lawsuits against a chain of for-profits called ITT and California-based Ashford University. The U.S. Department of Education is also revising its practices to stanch the flow of federal student loans to predatory for-profit colleges.

Since federal loans constitute about 85% of all outstanding education loan debt, what the federal government does in terms of public policy matters. Free or affordable higher education is now part of the progressive political discourse, addressing an issue of concern to millions of millennials and their parents. With their new political allies, student loan activists continue to lobby for specific changes in federal policy, including (1) allowing student loans to be renegotiated to take advantage of lower interest rates; (2) allowing student loans to be dischargeable in bankruptcy; (3) asking Congress and the U.S. Department of Education to lower interest rates to zero or just enough to cover the costs of default; (4) increasing options for income-based repayment; (5) seeking debt forgiveness after 10 (or 20) years of steady, on-time payments;

and (6) demanding for more grant aid and other means to enable free or very low-cost public higher education. These measures would ensure that the federal government does not seek to profit from public provisioning of student loans. They would restructure the contract between student borrowers and federal (as well as private) lenders, by providing the kinds of safety nets available to other types of debtors.

The Campaign Continues

The establishment of land grant colleges, federal financial aid programs, and other legislative measures at the end of the nineteenth through the mid-twentieth century USA signified that investment in higher education was viewed as a public good. More than an individual investment aimed at improving lifetime earnings, affordable higher education met the public purposes of increasing class and race mobility, investing in human capital infrastructure, and enhancing macroeconomic growth. The benefits of an educated populace were socialized or shared. Costs, therefore, were also socialized.

Fifty years later, we have an altogether different story. Students are told that a college degree is necessary to compete in today's labor market, and those who do complete their education generally have higher wages, lower unemployment, and more job stability. But tuition has risen as middle class incomes have stagnated. State government subsidies and federal grants for low-income students have not kept pace with costs. The costs of higher education are increasingly privatized. This regressive institutional change is the structural basis for the ballooning student debt bubble.

Student loan activists, including leaders who forged their critique of the power of financial interests during the Occupy Wall Street protest, have risen up to challenge the new debt bubble. Using tactics such as collective debt strikes and crowdfunding debt forgiveness, student debtors have challenged the morality of social norms that pose debt as an individual choice and an individual burden. Instead, they have redirected the conversation to a structural critique of the institutional arrangements for provisioning higher education. This critique has already led to the federal government assuming the role of lender in the primary market for students loans—a dramatic step toward institutional reform. Regulators are curbing abusive practices by for-profit colleges, lenders, and loan servicers.

This reinvigorated movement for progressive institutional change highlights the direct link between the question of how education is financed and democratic access. The predatory practices of the for-profit model of higher education provisioning and student loan servicers remind us that financialization reduces goods and services to instruments of speculation rather than means of enhancing well-being. Some goods and services need to be provisioned by institutions that embrace a public purpose. The public purpose of higher education can be better accomplished through institutional reforms that include direct government investment in public colleges and universities and the students who attend institutions of higher learning. The ultimate goal is social provisioning of higher education.

Notes

1. I thank Sandy Baum and his coauthors for granting permission to reproduce this figure from Ma et al. (2015). See also Baum (2016).
2. We cannot assume that students are borrowing in lieu of work. Data show that most students work in the paid labor market during college to help fund their education. Students graduating with debt have worked multiple jobs or more than 20 h per week (Huelsman 2016, Table 7). Also, the percent of Americans saving for college has increased from 31% in 2009 to 41% in 2015 (FINRA 2016, 18).
3. This includes psychological well-being. One recent study employs a five-question mental health inventory and finds that student loans are positively associated with poorer psychological functioning, in part due to stress and worries about repayment (Walsemann et al. 2015).
4. Four years after the federal government began to lend directly to students, in 2014, Sallie Mae split into two companies, and Navient took on the loan servicing part of the business. Sallie Mae remains a financial services company.
5. My summary of debt strike activities draws from the work of Hannah Appel (2014, 2015a), who spent considerable time at Occupy Wall Street and made field notes, Pamela Brown (2014), one of the founders of Strike Debt, and Anya Kamenetz (2015).
6. Effective December of 2015, the U.S. Department of Education made a new repayment plan for federal student loan borrowers available, called REPAYE. This is the most helpful plan to date, covering all prior borrowers. It limits monthly loan payments to 10% of discretionary income and forgives any remaining balance after 20 years of regular payments.

Supplementary Applications

1. Visit the Project on Student Debt website for the latest data on average debt for student borrowers. Compare the average student loan debt of graduates for your college or university to the average in your state and the average in the U.S.
2. On the Bureau of Labor Statistics website, find news releases for the Consumer Price Index (CPI-U). Drill down into the tables to find the percent change in "college tuition and fees" and contrast this with the percent change with other key products and services. You may want to do this for several months of data in a row or year-over-year changes taking a month such as June.
3. Locate on YouTube the video titled *Default: the Student Loan Documentary* (27 min), also available at http://www.defaultmovie.com/. This film originally aired on PBS television stations in the U.S. in October of 2011. It covers the history of student loans and the loan crisis through the lenses of borrowers from different backgrounds. A companion to the film would include *Generation Debt* by Anna Kamenetz (2006), a book by a millennial for the millennial generation. Discuss ways in which borrower student loan debt balances balloon (increase), even after someone has graduated college. The film concludes with student protests and policy implications. Which current policies do you argue should be adopted or changed?

References

Appel, Hannah. 2014. Occupy Wall Street and the Economic Imagination. *Cultural Anthropology* 29 (4): 602–625.

Appel, Hannah. 2015a. You Are Not a Loan: Strike Debt and the Emerging Debtors Movement. *Tikkun* 30 (1): 28–30.

Appel, Hannah. 2015b. The Idea Life of Money and Poststructural Realism. *HAU: Journal of Ethnographic Theory* 5 (2): 427–433.

Austin, Daniel A. 2013. The Indentured Generation: Bankruptcy and Student Loan Debt. *Santa Clara Law Review* 53 (2): 329–420.

Baum, Sandy. 2015. The Evolution of Student Debt in the United States. In *Student Loans and the Dynamics of Debt*, ed. Brad Hershbein and Kevin Hollenbeck, 11–35. Kalamazoo, MI: W.E. Upjohn Institute for Employment Research.

Baum, Sandy. 2016. *Student Debt: Rhetoric and Realities of Higher Education Funding*. New York: Palgrave Macmillan.

Best, Joel, and Eric Best. 2014. *The Student Loan Mess: How Good Intentions Created a Trillion-Dollar Problem*. Berkeley: University of California Press.

Brown, Pamela. 2014. When Theory Meets Heart: The Rolling Jubilee as a New Methodology for Debt Resistance. *Occasion* 7, 6 November. http://arcade.stanford.edu/occasion/when-theory-meets-heart-rolling-jubilee-and-lessons-occupying-debt.

Carey, Kevin. 2015. Student Debt in America: Lend With a Smile, Collect with a Fist. *New York Times*, 27 November.

Cellini, Stephanie Riegg, and Rajeev Darolia. 2015. College Costs and Financial Constraints: Student Borrowing at For-Profit Institutions. In *Student Loans and the Dynamics of Debt*, ed. Brad Hershbein and Kevin Hollenbeck, 137–173. Kalamazoo, MI: W.E. Upjohn Institute for Employment Research.

Consumer Finance Protection Bureau (CFPB). 2015a. CFPB Secures $480 Million in Debt Relief for Current and Former Corinthian Students. News Release (3 February). http://www.consumerfinance.gov/newsroom/cfpb-secures-480-million-in-debt-relief-for-current-and-former-corinthian-students/.

Consumer Finance Protection Bureau (CFPB). 2015b. *Annual Report of the CFPB Student Loan Ombudsman*. Washington, DC: CFPB.

Financial Investor Education Foundation (FINRA). 2016. Financial Capability in the United States. http://www.usfinancialcapability.org/.

Fry, Richard. 2012. *A Record One-in-Five Households Now Owe Student Loan Debt*. 26 September. Washington, DC: Pew Research Center.

Goldrick-Rab, Sara, and Robert Kelchen. 2015. Making Sense of Loan Aversion: Evidence from Wisconsin. In *Student Loans and the Dynamics of Debt*, ed. Brad Hershbein and Kevin Hollenbeckm, 317–377. Kalamazoo, MI: W.E. Upjohn Institute for Employment Research.

Hampton, Paul A. 2015. Power Without the King: The Debt Strike as Credible Threat. *Tikkun* 30 (1): 31–34.

Houle, Jason N. 2013. Disparities in Debt: Parents' Socioeconomic Resources and Young Adult Student Loan Debt. *Sociology of Education* 87 (1): 53–69.

Huelsman, Mark. 2016. *A Leg Up: How a Privileged Minority Is Graduating Without Debt*. Washington, DC: Dēmos.

Izzo, Phil. 2013. Number of the Week: Class of 2013 Most Indebted Ever. *Wall Street Journal* blog Real Time Economics, 18 May. http://blogs.wsj.com/economics/2013/05/18/number-of-the-week-class-of-2013-most-indebted-ever/.

Jackson, Brandon A., and John R. Reynolds. 2013. The Price of Opportunity: Race, Student Loan Debt, and College Achievement. *Sociological Inquiry* 83 (3): 335–368.

Kamenetz, Anya. 2015. Activists Stop Paying Their Student Loans, 31 March. http://www.npr.org/sections/ed/2015/03/31/396585597/activists-stop-paying-their-student-loans.

Looney, Adam, and Constantine Yannelis. 2015. *A Crisis in Student Loans? How Changes in the Characteristics of Borrowers and in the Institutions They Attended Contributed to Rising Loan Defaults.* 10–11 September. Washington, DC: Brookings Institution, BPEA Conference Draft.

Ma, Jennifer, Sandy Baum, Matea Pender, and D'Wayne Bell. 2015. *Trends in College Pricing 2015.* New York: College Board.

Marez, Curtis. 2014. Seeing in the Red: Looking at Student Debt. *American Quarterly* 66 (2): 261–281.

Nguyen, Mary. 2012. Degreeless in Debt: What Happens to Borrowers Who Drop Out? http://educationpolicy.air.org/sites/default/files/publications/DegreelessDebt_CYCT_RELEASE.pdf.

Ratcliffe, Caroline, and Signe-Mary McKernan. 2013. *Forever in Your Debt: Who Has Student Loan Debt, and Who's Worried?* Washington, DC: The Urban Institute.

Shafer, Joseph. 2015. Academic Publishing on Student Debt: Homo Academicus Americanus. *Inquiry Sanglap: Journal of Literary and Cultural* 1 (2): 127–148.

Strike Debt. 2014. *Debt Resistors' Operations Manual.* Oakland, CA: PM Press.

The Pew Charitable Trusts. 2015. *Federal and State Funding of Higher Education: A Changing Landscape.* Washington, DC: Pew.

U.S. Government Accountability Office (GAO). 2014. *Higher Education: State Funding Trends and Policies on Affordability.* Washington, DC (GAO-15-151).

U.S. Senate, Committee on Health, Education, Labor, and Pensions. 2012. *For Profit Higher Education: The Failure to Safeguard the Federal Investment and Ensure Student Success.* 30 July. Washington, DC (S-PRT. 112-137).

Walsemann, Katrina M., Gilbert C. Lee, and Danielle Gentile. 2015. Sick of Our Loans: Student Borrowing and the Mental Health of Young Adults in the United States. *Social Science & Medicine* 124: 85–93.

CHAPTER 8

Transforming Legal Rights and Social Values: Marriage Redefined

Abstract The path to marriage equality in the USA progressed—like previous civil rights moments—over decades, sometimes in waves but at other times with backlash. The movement for marriage equality (the redefinition of the institution of marriage) can be viewed as a rejection of invidious distinctions between the romantic unions of straight couples and gay couples. This story spotlights four moments in legal history culminating with the *Obergefell v. Hodges* Supreme Court decision on June 26, 2015, legalizing marriage equality nationwide. These legal strategies worked in tandem with state legislation as well as other forms of activism. The analysis shows that courts do not operate in a vacuum. They are both influenced by and influence society and its changing values, with iterative feedback effects.

Keywords Marriage equality · Constitutional law · Civil unions LGBTQ rights

JEL Codes J12 · J18 · J78 · K36

In 1970, two men who applied for a marriage license in a county clerk's office in Minneapolis, Minnesota, were denied. Their legal challenge was dismissed by the trial court, upheld by the state supreme court, and the U.S. Supreme Court refused to hear the case. More than 40 years later, on June 26 in 2013 and 2015, respectively, the U.S. Supreme Court struck down the Defense of Marriage Act (DOMA) in *Windsor v. United States* and declared that same-sex marriage is a constitutional right in *Obergefell v. Hodges*. As Supreme Court Justice Anthony Kennedy noted in his landmark *Obergefell* decision, "[t]he history of marriage is one of both continuity and change." Furthermore, "[f]ar from seeking to devalue marriage, the petitioners seek it for themselves because of their respect—and need—for its privileges and responsibilities" (*Obergefell v. Hodges*, 6, 4). Nevertheless, it would be too simplistic to characterize these victories as stemming from these two sole Supreme Court cases, or even their brave lawyers and plaintiffs.

The path to marriage equality progressed—like previous civil rights moments—over decades, sometimes in waves and other times with backlash. As attorney-activist and Freedom to Marry founder Evan Wolfson has said: "[w]e didn't come to this movement overnight" (as quoted in Ball 2015). Instead, the recognition of full (federal) marriage equality in the USA is a multidimensional, nuanced story of institutional domains for contesting the definition of marriage: courts, legislatures, ballot referenda, grassroots campaigns and public pressure, individual actors and their families, and businesses and other organizations. Also fundamental was the shift of public opinion from minority to majority support for marriage equality over a period of about 10 years, buttressed by changes in popular culture, including the sympathetic portrayal of gay characters on television and in film. Finally, economic interests gradually shifted, as large corporations looked for uniformity in human resource policies across state lines and businesses came to recognize same-sex couples as an emerging market.

This chapter is a story about the progressive institutional change surrounding the redefinition of the institution of marriage. The achievement of legal marriage equality in the United States can be viewed as a rejection of invidious distinctions between the romantic unions of straight couples and gay couples. Others might focus on the ceremonial function of marriage linked to religious rites that solemnify a couple's relationship with a particular community of believers. While not negating the symbolic importance of the ceremonial aspects of marriage for the individuals involved, advocates for marriage equality more often focus on its instrumental value for families, communities, and nations.

As one example, there are practical reasons for gay men and lesbians to seek inclusion into the institution of marriage. According to historian

George Chauncey in *Why Marriage?* a book based in part on interviews with gay couples, even when accepted by friends and family, gay men and lesbians felt their relationships were vulnerable. Treatment by both public and private institutions is linked to marital status. For example, marriage has more than 1000 federal benefits tied to it. Gay rights attorney Mary Bonauto (2005, 6) has argued: "[T]he fifty dollars a couple spends on a marriage license will buy them more protection than any set of lawyers' documents ever will." The terrain of this illustration of institutional change thus centers on laws regulating marriage. Legal decisions played a key role in redefining marriage, and also in nudging public opinion.[1]

Four Legal Milestones

This story of marriage equality spotlights four key moments in legal history as the impetus for state legislation as well as activism. On the eve of the *Obergefell* decision, gay marriage had already been made legal in 36 US states. Eleven state legislatures had passed marriage equality laws subsequently signed by governors, and 25 other states had achieved marriage equality as a result of court decisions. Fourteen states had constitutional amendments banning gay marriage, under challenge in the *Obergefell* case. The four key moments are:

- On May 5, 1993, in *Baehr v. Lewin*, Hawaii's supreme court became the first in the nation to rule that denying marriage to same-sex couples violates the equal protection clause of the state constitution, but the decision was quickly undermined.
- On November 17, 2003, Massachusetts became the first state to legalize same-sex marriage following a ruling in its state supreme court in the case of *Goodridge v. Department of Public Health*.
- On June 26, 2013, the U.S. Supreme Court overturned the federal Defense of Marriage Act (or DOMA, a law that allowed states to refuse to recognize same-sex marriage and made heterosexual marriages the only ones recognized under federal law) in *Windsor v. United States*, and dismissed a challenge to California's Proposition 8—the successful statewide ballot initiative to roll back marriage equality—in *Hollingsworth v. Perry*.
- June 26, 2015, U.S. Supreme Court affirmed marriage equality nationwide in *Obergefell v. Hodges*, stating that the equal protection clause of the Fourteenth Amendment to the U.S. Constitution

requires states to issue marriage licenses to same-sex couples and recognize marriages from other states.

Many civil rights groups were working on various cases in the two decades prior to the victories in *Windsor* (2013) and *Obergefell* (2015). These court cases were filed by individual civil rights lawyers, usually working with gay rights legal groups. The *Baehr* case in Hawaii, for example, was filed by a private attorney, with Lambda Legal Defense and Education Fund's Evan Wolfson joined as co-counsel. Mary Bonauto worked for Gay & Lesbian Advocates and Defenders (GLAD) in Boston and had filed a case that supported marriage over Vermont civil unions even before she represented the *Goodridge* plaintiffs in Massachusetts (see Bonauto et al. 2016). She also challenged DOMA in several cases that worked their way slowly through the courts. Corporate attorney Roberta Kaplan filed *Windsor*, but she had long ties to the American Civil Liberties Union's (ACLU) LGBT & AIDS Project. In addition, Kaplan teamed with Mary Bonauto, who organized the amicus briefs for *Windsor*. And Mary Bonauto (and Douglas Hallward-Driemier) soon argued *Obergefell v. Hodges*, aided by the ACLU of Ohio and other private attorneys.

Courts do not operate in a vacuum, though. Behind these individual attorneys and their individual clients were gay rights legal groups, their activist members, and allies and advocates.[2] Even when the tactical focus was on convincing the courts to reinterpret the law, advances required a significant social movement in pursuit of institutional change. Laws are influenced by society. But there are also iterative feedback effects as laws reshape social norms and thus society itself.

FROM BEGINNINGS TO *BAEHR* TO BACKLASH

The gay rights movement was still relatively young at the time of the *Baehr* case in Hawaii in 1993. Philadelphia's Independence Hall was the site of the first, very small demonstration (about 40 people) against discrimination, igniting the national gay rights movement on July 4, 1965. The uprising and resistance to police brutality at a raid on June 28, 1969, at the Stonewall Inn, a gay bar in Greenwich Village in New York City, is more generally seen as the spark in the movement. Ten years later in 1979, some 100,000 people gathered on the Capitol Mall for the first National March on Washington for Lesbian and Gay Rights. Four additional marches followed in 1987, 1993, 2000, and 2009. Marriage was not the top priority in the early movement, viewed as an unrealistic and particularly controversial demand.

Gays and lesbians faced discrimination in housing and employment. The AIDS crisis in the 1980s and 1990s left partners without access to hospital visitation with and/or the ability to make medical decisions for their loved ones, and without inheritance rights. Private sexual activity between same-sex partners could be prosecuted in many states until the U.S. Supreme Court struck down Texas' anti-sodomy law in *Lawrence v. Texas* in 2003. In another significant victory for gay rights, in *Romer v. Evans* in 1996, the U.S. Supreme Court struck down a voter-approved amendment to the Colorado state constitution that overturned city gay rights ordinances and forbid either cities or the state from enacting such measures in the future. The *Lawrence* and *Romer* decisions were critical building blocks for later marriage rulings.

The three Hawaii couples who sued for same sex marriage in 1991 lost in a lower court. On appeal, they won a pyrrhic victory. The state Supreme Court found that denying marriage licenses to same-sex couples constituted discrimination based on sex, requiring justification under a legal standard known as strict scrutiny. But it remanded the *Baehr* case back to the trial court to determine whether there was a compelling state interest to justify denying marriage licenses to gay couples. If so, that standard would be satisfied and denial would not be viewed as abridging constitutional rights.

The Hawaiian decision resulted in severe backlash (see Klarman 2012), prompting state legislators to propose an amendment to the state's constitution to ban same-sex marriage. It was ratified overwhelmingly by Hawaii voters in 1998 (with 69% in favor). Then-President Bill Clinton signed the federal Defense of Marriage Act (DOMA) in 1996, leaving it up to US states to decide whether to recognize same-sex marriages legally performed in other states and countries around the world. A majority of states eventually barred recognition of gay marriage via "defense of marriage laws" or executive orders, 29 in total between 1996 and 1999. Marriage equality seemed more remote than ever.

In the *Baehr* era, gay men and lesbians could not serve openly in the US military and, if their sexuality was discovered, they could be discharged for it. As a presidential candidate in 1992, Bill Clinton campaigned on a plank to remove all discrimination against those serving openly in the military. Once elected, however, he signed on to an unsatisfactory compromise passed by the U.S. Congress in 1993 called "Don't Ask, Don't Tell" (DADT). A gay serviceperson could serve as long as they were not open about their sexual orientation and as long as their sexual identity was not brought to the attention of superiors. Though DADT was a moderation of previous US policy, the military continued to engage in investigations and order dismissals. DADT was later repealed by the U.S. Congress in a 2010 law signed by President Barak Obama.

Legal Strategy Shifts: Massachusetts and California

The first decade of the 2000s brought with it fresh advances and continuing setbacks. Private companies recognized gay spouses for benefits long before the federal and state governments required them to do so. The Human Rights Campaign (HRC) began publishing its annual Corporate Equality Index, a benchmarking tool of company policies for LGBTs (lesbians, gays, bisexuals, and transgender people), in 2002. The Netherlands legalized gay marriage in 2000, the first country in the world to do so. In the early 2000s, civil rights attorneys nationwide were coalescing around the position that a cornucopia of legal documents—powers of attorney, health care proxies, creative co-parent adoptions, and wills and trusts—would not provide the full benefits of marriage. At the same time, state after state continued to pass DOMAs, defining marriage as between one man and one woman and refusing to recognize any same-sex marriage performed in another state or country.

After *Baehr*, the network of advocates became more strategic. Attorneys at organizations like Lambda Legal Defense and Education Fund and Gay & Lesbian Advocates and Defenders (GLAD) carefully studied the language in state constitutions, state discrimination and hate crimes legislation, and opinions of judges on state supreme courts to assess whether they would have a high likelihood of prevailing—and not being overturned by constitutional amendment, as in Hawaii. The campaign started with Vermont. Three same-sex couples who were denied marriage licenses filed suit, represented by Boston-based GLAD attorney Mary Bonauto and two attorneys from Vermont. In *Baker v. Vermont* (1999), the supreme court of the state ruled that the exclusion of same-sex couples from marriage violated the state's constitution's provision, guaranteeing "the common benefit, protection, and security of the people" (quoted in Klarman 2012, 76). The court charged the legislature with correcting the discrimination and conferring to same-sex couples the same rights and benefits as married couples. Eschewing the word "marriage", Vermont invented what we know as "civil unions" in 2000.

In Massachusetts, Gay & Lesbian Advocates and Defenders (GLAD) filed the *Goodridge* case in 2001 with Mary Bonauto as lead attorney. The *Goodridge* case was not a bolt out of the blue, according to Bonauto (2015), as the Massachusetts legislature and state courts had been gradually adding to the rights of gay citizens, including passage of non-discrimination laws and a hate crimes law. There were seven couples in the case. Some plaintiffs had biological and/or adopted children, some had health problems or had lost spouses to long illnesses, some had been denied hospital visitations or end-of-life caretaking decisions. In other words, behind these cases were stories of real families with real challenges. This strategy worked in Massachusetts and was followed in other cases.

After November 17, 2003, when the Massachusetts court issued its decision in favor of same-sex marriage in *Goodridge*, anti-gay groups and then-Massachusetts Governor Mitt Romney tried many ploys to delay its implementation. But advocates fought back. That is when Coretta Scott King publicly linked LGBT rights with civil rights. Although criticized by black pastors, she stood firm. In a speech at Stockton University—my home institution—on March 23, 2004, King said that same-sex marriage was a civil rights issue. After Massachusetts began gay weddings in May 2004, a wave of eleven states passed DOMA-type ballot initiatives the following November—a political strategy that turned out conservative voters during a presidential election year. More ballot measures banning recognition of same-sex marriages passed in successive November general elections. Yet the reality of the Massachusetts experience was a profoundly important moment. Massachusetts residents, and people around the country, witnessed happy couples celebrating their nuptials, with no dire impact.

It took 4 years after the *Goodridge* decision in Massachusetts for California to become the second marriage equality state in 2008. Once again, Americans watched a rush to the alter by ecstatic couples, as the state supreme court ruled that excluding same-sex couples from marriage was unconstitutional. Opposition groups quickly mobilized in response, collecting signatures for Proposition 8. "Prop 8" was an amendment to the state constitution that restricted marriage to heterosexual couples. The measure passed 52–48% in November, the same day that Barack Obama carried California on his way to winning the presidency. Abruptly, marriage licenses stopped being issued in the state. Fears that the marriages already performed during the brief window would be annulled led to a period of legal limbo that ultimately preserved the existing unions. Court victories were more permanent in two other states, Connecticut in 2008 and Iowa in 2009. Still, a decade of slow advances in the courts was coupled with defeats at the ballot box with the expansion of state DOMAs. Clearly, advocates could not seek justice through the courts alone.

THE COURT OF PUBLIC OPINION

It became increasingly apparent that advocates could not rely solely on the courts for marriage equality. The movement needed political as well as legal victories. The public had to support gay marriage at the polls or through their state representatives (Ball 2015). Nevertheless, the legal strategies created the cultural image of joyous weddings in some states contrasted with tragic stories of cold-hearted policies in other states that helped the activists shape public opinion. The backlash against Proposition eight in California seemed to be louder and stronger than the initial backlash that led to its passage in the first place.

Freedom to Marry, founded in 2003 by lawyer-turned-activist Evan Wolfson, focused on coordinating political campaigns to win marriage equality. The movement's successes picked up pace after 2008 as public opinion began to move in favor of marriage equality. With dedicated work by Freedom to Marry and networks of state activists, as well as the models of positive change in Massachusetts, Connecticut, and Iowa, state legislatures subsequently enacted marriage equality in the 11 states (and Washington, DC) listed in Table 8.1.

Since words matter, I had wondered at the time whether the increased use by activists and the media of the newer phrase "marriage equality"—with the emphasis on rights, as opposed to "same-sex marriage" or "gay marriage" with an implied stress on a sexual act or special treatment—helped to sway public opinion. I cannot locate any history of the phrase "marriage equality" or academic paper on my hypothesis. But clearly, ideas about marriage were steadily being redefined so that rather than separate categories—traditional versus same-sex marriage—the institution was being reframed to encompass broader forms.

The Gallup polling organization started tracking public support for marriage equality in 1996. The exact poll question was: "Do you think marriages between same-sex couples should or should not be recognized

Table 8.1 US states with marriage equality through legislation or ballot initiative

State	Year	Process
Vermont	2009	Legislature overrides Governor veto
Maine	2009 [2012][a]	Legislature, Governor, then Ballot
New Hampshire	2009	Legislature, Governor
Washington, DC	2009	City Council, Mayor
New York	2011	Legislature, Governor
Washington	2012	Legislature, Governor then Ballot reaffirms
Maryland	2012	Legislature, Governor then Ballot reaffirms
Minnesota	2012, 2013	Ballot, then Legislature, Governor
Rhode Island	2012	Legislature, Governor
Delaware	2013	Legislature, Governor
Hawaii	2013	Legislature, Governor
Illinois	2013	Legislature, Governor

[a]A subsequent ballot measure in Maine barred implementation until 2012 when a second ballot measure reversed the first
Source: Freedom to Marry website at http://www.freedomtomarry.org/pages/winning-in-the-states

by the law as valid, with the same rights as traditional marriages?" In March 1996, 27% of respondents agreed that such marriages should be valid (Gallup n.d.). By May 2015 it was 60%, having crossed the majority threshold in the May 2011 poll. In 2011, President Barack Obama ordered the U.S. Department of Justice to stop defending DOMA. And on May 9, 2012, President Obama came out in favor of marriage equality, which became part of the Democratic Party platform in September, the same (election) year. When the court ruled in favor of marriage equality in *Obergefell*, public support was about three times as high as when the court ruled in favor of interracial marriage in *Loving v. Virginia* in 1967 (Gallup 2013).

Justice that Arrives like a Thunderbolt

In retrospect, it is perhaps the third legal moment that was the most significant advance on the road to marriage equality: the 2013 decision in *Windsor v. United States*. The attorney for the case, Roberta Kaplan, wrote in a law journal the year before the decision that the litigation on DOMA (*Windsor*) "may well presage a gigantic leap forward for the principle of equal protection of the laws for gay men and lesbians" (Kaplan and Fink 2012, 1). By 2015, with the stage set by *Windsor*, the *Obergefell* decision—the fourth legal moment—did just that.

Kaplan filed *Windsor* in 2011. In 2006, she had lost a New York Supreme Court case for marriage equality on behalf of 13 gay couples. Years later Edith (Edie) Schlain Windsor, a retired IBM computer programmer, contacted her. Edie was charged $363,053 in federal inheritance taxes and $275,528 in New York State for the estate of her longtime partner, Thea Spyer. The two were legally married in Canada in 2007 (they had gotten secretly engaged in 1967). Edie took care of Thea during her long bout with multiple sclerosis, up to Thea's death in 2009. The couple was the center of a 2009 documentary film, "Edie and Thea: A Very Long Engagement" that was shown in film festivals around the world. Kaplan wanted to litigate DOMA and she thought it was important to have a client with a story that people and judges could connect with—as lawyers might say—an appealing litigant, an ideal plaintiff (these details are from Levy 2013 and Kaplan and Dickey 2015).

Oral arguments in the *Windsor* case went extremely well for the plaintiffs. In her questioning, Justice Ruth Bader Ginsburg characterized Edie's marriage under DOMA as a "skim milk marriage" as opposed to "full marriage." This both humorous and artful phrase helps us understand the invidious distinctions at stake. Kaplan later assessed Justice Anthony Kennedy's opinion in her behind-the-scenes look into the case, *Then Comes Marriage*: "What the *Windsor* opinion is about is human dignity and equality. Justice Kennedy wrote [in his majority opinion] that 'interference with the equal dignity of same-sex marriages was more than an incidental effect of DOMA. It was its essence.' He observed that 'DOMA writes inequality into the entire United States Code', commenting that DOMA 'touches many aspects of married and family life, from the mundane to the profound'" (Kaplan with Dickey 2015, 292–293).

The *Windsor* decision set off a "domino effect" (Ball 2015), as district courts and appellate courts drew on its reasoning to strike down the bans against same-sex marriage in state after state. In all but one of the numerous cases in the United States Courts of Appeals (the level immediately below the Supreme Court), the lower courts had found that excluding same-sex couples from marrying violates the U.S. Constitution. By 2015, when the U.S. Supreme Court heard the *Obergefell* case, only fourteen state marriage bans were left standing.

James Obergefell had lost his longtime partner, John Arthur, to Amyotrophic Lateral Sclerosis (ALS or "Lou Gehrig's Disease") in 2013. When John was very ill, they flew from Ohio to Maryland on a medical jet, married on the tarmac, and returned to Ohio to demand that their out-of-state legal marriage be recognized in life and on John's death certificate. It was not.

As *Obergefell* wound its way through the courts, it was combined with other cases, so that eventually there were 32 couples seeking constitutional recognition of marriage equality. The *Obergefell v. Hodges* decision was announced 2 years to the day after *Windsor*. Same-sex couples may now marry in all 50 US states and the District of Columbia. The United States was finally catching up in a world in which 17 countries had already legalized gay marriage, including Ireland (with Catholicism as the predominant religion), whose citizens had approved marriage equality in a referendum on May 22, 2015.

Both the *Windsor* and *Obergefell* decisions affirmed that denying equal protection to a group of people violates human dignity. As Roberta Kaplan reflects: "[i]n his opinion for the Court in *Windsor*, Justice Kennedy uses the word 'dignity' eleven times in 23 pages" (quoted in Grindley 2014). By my own count, the word dignity, including the phrase "dignitary wounds" appears 14 times in Justice Kennedy's 28-page decision in *Obergefell*. This emphasis on dignity in these two decisions reflects, I would argue, more than formal equality. It recognizes the need for social and economic institutions such as marriage to enable human flourishing.

Courts play a paramount role in my spotlight of four legal moments in the story of marriage equality for a reason. In 2005, Jon Davidson, legal director of the Lambda Legal Defense and Education Fund, argued during an address at Yale Law School that advances in legislatures and public opinion do matter, but that court decisions like *Goodridge* have propelled the biggest advances (Davidson 2005). Law professor Michael Klarman echoes this opinion: "*Goodridge* inspired gays not only to marry but also to litigate for gay marriage in other states" (2012, 178). Still, I believe that lasting advances happen only with evolving culture and public opinion, that is, pressure from outside the courts.[3]

As President Obama articulated in the White House Rose Garden on June 26, 2015, sometimes "a slow, steady effort is rewarded with justice that arrives like a thunderbolt." That is how justice arrived in this case. But it was not without warning, and it arrived when the conditions were ripe. All of the four legal moments arose out of earlier building blocks of both precedent and activism. The irony is that activists originally expected that marriage equality would be harder to achieve than equality in the public sphere, like housing and employment discrimination. The institutional rigidity of heterosexual marriage seemed daunting. In this story of institutional change, the laws regulating marriage reflected the invidious distinctions embedded in cultural norms. As the LGBT community developed a sense of its own agency, it set about to change those cultural norms, leading to a rereading of state constitutions and ultimately the U.S. Constitution. You have to change culture to change laws, but legal precedents also have a feedback effect in changing culture. As Daniel Bromley reflects in his 2016 Veblen-Commons address for the Association of Evolutionary Economics: "Actions of legislatures and courts redirect or reallocate economic opportunities for differently situated individuals. …but there can be no doubt that public policy is precisely concerned with such reallocations of relative advantage in the economy. This is what institutional change entails" (2016, 318).

Notes

1. My abbreviated account here has been informed by many academic sources, newspaper and magazine articles, books such as George Chauncey's *Why Marriage?* (2004), Michael Klarman's *From the Closet to the Altar* (2012), Kevin Cathcart and Leslie Gabel-Brett's *Love Unites Us* (2016), Debbie Cenziper and Jim Obergefell's *Love Wins* (2016), as well as law review articles (e.g., Duncan 2003; Bonauto 2005; Davidson 2005; Kaplan and Fink 2012).
2. The details of what led to the *Windsor* case through oral argument and victory celebrations are covered in Roberta Kaplan's own book, *Then Comes Marriage* (2015).
3. One model of progressive institutional change depicts ceremonial patterns of behavior displaced peacefully, through the involvement of these interests themselves in the problem-solving process that is beneficial for all participants (Hielscher et al. 2012). Especially in the case of marriage equality, I do not think that the process is necessarily a peaceful process that is well accepted, a settled habit of thought.

Supplementary Applications

1. After winning marriage equality in the U.S., gay rights activists have said that in the United States you can get married on a Saturday and still be fired from your job on a Monday. Not every U.S. state nor every employer's policy forbids employment discrimination on the basis of sexual orientation. The Employment Non-Discrimination Act (ENDA) has languished in the U.S. Congress. In brief, what is the history of the federal ENDA bill?
2. Which U.S. states forbid employment discrimination on the basis of sexual orientation? Is it for public sector employment only or both private and public sector jobs?
3. Which U.S. states forbid employment discrimination on the basis of gender identity or gender expression, for example, protecting transgender persons?
4. Visit the website of the Human Rights Campaign (HRC). Look at the section on the Corporate Equality Index. Review the criteria for companies to score well on the index. Find a couple of companies that are doing well on this index.

References

Baker v. Vermont, 744A. 2d 864 (VT. 1999), decided December 20, 1999.

Ball, Molly. 2015. How Gay Marriage Became a Constitutional Right. *The Atlantic*, July 1. http://www.theatlantic.com/politics/archive/2015/07/gay-marriage-supreme-court-politics-activism/397052/.

Bonauto, Mary L. 2005. Goodridge in Context. *Harvard Civil Rights-Civil Liberties Law Review* 40 (1): 1–69.

Bonauto, Mary (interviewed by Jo Ann Citron). 2015. Goodridge Takes Effect: Now What? The Gay and Lesbian Review. May-June. http://www.glreview.org/article/article-1327/.

Bonauto, Mary L., Gary D. Buseck, and Janson Wu. 2016. New Frontiers: State Legislative Wins and Federal DOMA Challenges. In *Love Unites Us: Winning the Freedom to Marry in America*, ed. Kevin M. Cathcart and Leslie J. Gabel-Brett, 181–194. New York, NY: The New Press.

Bromley, Daniel W. 2016. The 2016 Veblen-Commons Award Recipient: Daniel W. Bromley: Institutional Economics. *Journal of Economic Issues* 50 (2): 309–325.

Cathcart, Kevin M., and Leslie J. Gabel-Brett (eds.). 2016. *Love Unites Us: Winning the Freedom to Marry in America*. New York: The New Press.

Cenziper, Debbie, and Jim Obergefell. 2016. *Love Wins: The Lovers and Lawyers Who Fought for the Landmark Case for Marriage Equity*. New York: William Morrow.

Chauncey, George. 2004. *Why Marriage? The History Shaping Today's Debate Over Gay Equality*. New York: Basic Books.

Davidson, Jon W. 2005. Winning Marriage Equality: Lessons from Court. *Yale Journal of Law and Feminism* 17 (1): 297–308.

Duncan, William C. 2003. The Litigation to Redefine Marriage: Equality and Social Meaning. *Brigham Young University Journal of Public Law* 18 (2): 623–663.

Freedom to Marry. n.d. Winning the States. http://www.freedomtomarry.org/pages/winning-in-the-states.

Gallup. n.d.Marriage. http://www.gallup.com/poll/117328/marriage.aspx.

Gallup. 2013. In U.S. 87% Approve of Black-White Marriage vs. 4% in 1958. http://www.gallup.com/poll/163697/approve-marriage-blacks-whites.aspx.

Grindley, Lucas. 2014. In Her Own Words: Roberta Kaplan Remembers How DOMA Fell. *Advocate*, February 12. http://www.advocate.com/politics/marriage-equality/2014/02/12/her-own-words-roberta-kaplan-remembers-how-doma-fell.

Hielscher, Stefan, Ingo Pies, and Vladislav Valentinov. 2012. How to Foster Social Progress: An Ordonomic Perspective on Progressive Institutional Change. *Journal of Economic Issues* 46 (3): 779–797.

Kaplan, Roberta A., and Julie E. Fink. 2012. The Defense of Marriage Act: The Application of Heightened Scrutiny to Discrimination on the Basis of Sexual Orientation. *Cardozo Law Review de novo*: 203–213. http://www.cardozolawreview.com/debullnovo-archives.html.

Kaplan, Roberta, with Lisa Dickey. 2015. *Then Comes Marriage: United States v. Windsor and the Defeat of DOMA*. New York: W.W. Norton & Company.

Klarman, Michael J. 2012. *From the Closet to the Altar: Courts, Backlash, and the Struggle for Same-Sex Marriage*. New York: Oxford University Press.

Levy, Ariel. 2013. The Perfect Wife. *The New Yorker*, September 30.

Obergefell v. Hodges, No 14-556, decided June 26, 2015

United States v. Windsor, No 12-307, decided June 26, 2013.

CHAPTER 9

Greening the Economy: Certified Sustainable Coffee

Abstract About 1.6 billion cups of coffee are consumed every day around the world. Measured by trade volume, coffee is the most important agricultural crop. It is the second most traded commodity after oil. It was also the first product to be fair trade certified and is the leading global fair trade product. Shade-grown coffee, in particular, provides an alternative to agricultural practices that erode soil, over-utilize water, and decimate forest habitats. The shade-grown Rainforest Alliance and Smithsonian Migratory Bird Center bird-friendly coffees are featured. These certifications result from alliances between producers in the developing world and consumers in the USA and Europe. As described in this chapter, such certifications, though sometimes compromised, move us toward global sustainable agriculture and sustainable development practices.

Keywords Fair trade · Coffee production · Sustainable development · Ethical consumption · Green products

JEL Codes F13 · F18 · F64 · E21 · L13 · O13 · Q1

I do not drink coffee. But millions and millions of people do. About 1.6 billion cups of coffee are consumed every day around the world. Measured by trade volume, coffee is the most important agricultural crop. It is the second most traded commodity after oil (petroleum). It was also the first product to be fair trade certified and is the leading global fair trade product. Beginning in the Netherlands under the Max Havelaar brand in 1988 (Fridell 2007; Pay 2009), fair trade coffee has been increasingly available as an ethical choice for production and consumption. The term *fair trade* is intended as a direct contrast with neoliberalism's embrace of *free trade*. Fair trade is defined by the World Fair Trade Organization (n.d.) as "a trading partnership, based on dialogue, transparency and respect, that seeks greater equity in international trade. It contributes to sustainable development by offering better trading conditions to, and securing the rights of, marginalized producers and workers—especially in the [global] South." Fair trade coffee has become a symbolic product in contemporary movements to "green" the economy, that is, to minimize the destructive environmental consequences of production and consumption.

According to the International Trade Centre (ITC), a joint agency of the World Trade Organization and the United Nations, certified fair trade coffee had an 8% market share of worldwide sales in 2009. Yet fair trade-certified coffee is going mainstream at accelerating growth rates. Standard-compliant (fair trade) coffee production grew 26% per year from 2008 to 2012 (Potts et al. 2014, 160). In contrast, demand for conventional (non-certified) coffee is "largely stagnant" in the mature markets of the European Union, the United States, and Japan (Pierrot et al. 2011, 1). By 2012, 40% of global coffee was *produced* in compliance with a voluntary sustainability standard; unfortunately, only 25% was *sold* as standard compliant (Potts et al. 2014, 158).[1] Within and across countries, the difference between the production and consumption represents an oversupply. This can put downward pressure on prices (bad news for producers) while providing considerable choices for sustainable sourcing for large buyers in the USA and Europe.

Greening the economy will require more than simply changing the tastes and preferences of individual consumers so that they pay for fair trade products—though this is one component of the process. Fair trade networks, certifications and recognized standards, and practices such as eco-labeling are also aimed at transforming production processes by altering value structures on the supply side. As producers collectively organize to offer certified "green" products, the proliferation of labels and logos raises the awareness of consumers. Peter Söderbaum gives an example about fair trade coffee in Sweden and other European countries, where eco-labeling has become institutionalized via widely accepted trademarks and logos: "In the case of coffee, the idea of fair trade means that some consumers in Sweden are no longer exclusively interested in a price as low as possible for a given quality of coffee. They also take an interest in the way coffee is produced, for instance, with respect to environmental, health, and social impacts" (2000, 442). Changing values on the demand side, so that other things matter besides price and quality, thus interacts in a cumulative causation with the supply side.[2]

Institutionalist economist John Kenneth Galbraith identified a concept called the *dependence effect* in his 1958 book *The Affluent Society*. This concept refers to the seemingly self-evident idea that the development of consumer wants, tastes, and preferences is an economic process that economists should interrogate. Galbraith himself was particularly interested in the role of advertising in escalating consumption levels. The dependence effect, however, can be applied to analyzing the process of growing the market for fair trade and sustainably produced goods. Logos represent a kind of advertising that spark awareness and transform value structures.

This chapter presents the role of fair trade coffee in advancing the goal of sustainable development. After introducing the myriad certifications for fair trade coffee, I feature two certifications of shade-grown coffee: Rainforest Alliance (RA) and Smithsonian Migratory Bird Center (SMBC) Bird Friendly. These certifications result from alliances between producers in the developing world and consumers in the USA and Europe. As described in this chapter, such certifications, though sometimes compromised, move us toward global sustainable agriculture and sustainable development practices. But first we explore "why coffee?" and its relationship to a rejection of economic "growth" in favor of "sustainable development."

The Movement for Sustainable Development Emerges

The history of coffee certification is linked to the story of *sustainable development* as a concept and movement. Or, as environmental scientists Thomas Dietsch and Stacy Philpott argue, "Efforts to counter ecological and socio-economic degradation have put coffee at the forefront of a new sustainability movement to reform negative globalization trends" (2008, 247). During the neoliberal era, the dominant prescription for developing countries has been export-led economic growth. Oftentimes the export sectors of these economies are oriented around agriculture, particularly a single crop targeted for global markets.

Coffee is a prime example. Coffee is key to foreign exchange for the more than 50 countries that produce it. Fair trade advocates claim that coffee production actually intensifies poverty for producers in the global south. Producing for global markets is, in many ways, riskier than subsistence farming. First, the coffee market itself can be subject to much price volatility due to supply-side factors such as climate and speculation. Further, small-scale producers have little bargaining power in the global supply chain. They face an oligopolistic market of big coffee roasters and big coffee retailers, the latter of which are typically multinational corporations. The classical economic model of international trade focused on comparative advantage—an approach that found its way into Structural Adjustment Policies (SAP) supported by the World Bank and International Monetary Fund—assumes all parties benefit equally from trade. In general, producers of primary goods such as coffee have not benefited proportionately; as incomes rise in industrialized countries, demand for primary goods has lagged the swollen demand for industrial goods. Developing countries, therefore, suffer from declining terms of trade. A key moment occurred when a longstanding International Coffee Agreement (ICA) that established quotas to prop up prices collapsed in 1989 (Messier 2010). An oversupply of coffee and plummeting farmer incomes were like the straw that broke the camel's back. It nurtured a budding social justice movement in coffee production.

In addition to the economic power imbalances, there are environmental drawbacks of such single-sector or single-crop dependence, as noted by agroecologist Miguel Altieri, "[T]his type of industrial agriculture also brings a variety of economic, environmental, and social problems, including negative impacts on public health, ecosystem integrity, food quality, and in many cases disruption of traditional rural livelihoods, while accelerating indebtedness among thousands of farmers" (2009, 102). For example, it takes 30 gallons of water to grow coffee beans and process them to make one cup of standard American coffee, a little more for a European cup or an espresso. While rural populations suffer from hunger and poverty, the land is converted from local food production to export-oriented agribusiness in the name of development. Deforestation, in order to create large farm tracts for agribusiness, compounds a variety of environmental problems including climate change, vulnerability to floods, and disruption to habitats of migratory birds and other fauna.

Sustainable development, in contrast, supports the twin goals of human development and ecological balance. The collaborative work of local farmers, non-governmental organizations (NGOs), retailers, governments around the world, supported by increasing consumer awareness about what is in their "cup a joe," is creating alternative institutions for the production and distribution of coffee. The good news is that institutional practices are changing, with positive outcomes. Altieri (2009) argues that nearly two decades of agroecological invention have begun to effectuate a measured, positive impact on environmental conditions.

After years of planning, in 1992 world leaders met at the United Nations (UN) Conference on Environment and Development in Rio de Janeiro, Brazil (Rio Summit, also known as the "Earth Summit"). At the Earth Summit, a blueprint called Agenda 21 set priorities and advised practices in all economic and social sectors and further how they should relate to the environment (see Petty 2009). In hindsight, the summit likely played a role in helping popularize "sustainability" as a noun in policy discussions and "sustainable" as an adjective modifying the phrase economic development or economic growth. According to Agenda 21, "The overall human settlement objective is to improve the social economic and environmental quality of human settlements and the living and working environments of all people, in particular the urban and rural poor" (UN 1992, paragraph 7.4). Food security—adequate food and culturally appropriate food—is vital, of course, but in a sustainable fashion.

As part of Agenda 21, governments agreed to redirect policy to take account of environmental impact. Environmental mainstreaming, or considering the environment when evaluating any economic policy or practice, became part of development planning at the national and local levels. A specific objective was to rethink economic development agendas by finding ways to curb pollution and halt or slow destruction of the natural environment. The words "sustainable" and "sustainability" appear throughout Agenda 21. For example, governments should:

> [M]ake international trade and environment policies mutually supportive in favour of sustainable development. (UN 1992, paragraph 2.21a)

> Ensure that environmental policies provide the appropriate legal and institutional framework to respond to new needs for the protection of the

environment that may result from changes in production and trade specialization. (UN 1992, paragraph 2.221)

[I]ntegrate sustainable development considerations with agricultural policy analysis and planning in all countries, particularly in developing countries. (UN 1992, paragraph 14.5)

Global leaders decided to promote sustainable agriculture, accenting the management of water resources, toxic chemicals, hazardous wastes, and solid wastes (see also UN 1992, Chaps. 18 through 21).

Though not technically binding on national governments, the Rio Earth Summit subsequently played a significant role in bringing attention to policy measures by national governments as well as global activism by NGOs. Export-led growth can inhibit countries from acting unilaterally because global markets tend to undermine strong regulations by enforcing the drive to lower costs. To counter these pressures, the collaboration of NGOs working across borders with participants in the supply chain is institutionalizing these agreements. And the UN Food and Agricultural Organization (FAO) stays apprised of agricultural sustainability projects in dozens of countries. These voluntary efforts helped fuel a new discourse about sustainable development that influenced the fair trade movement.

Overlapping Definitions of Fair Trade-Certified Coffee

Fair trade is a voluntary labeling initiative with a goal of improving the livelihoods of small producers (farmers) and workers by offering better terms to producers, mostly poor farmers in developing countries. Some, but not all, fair trade standards incorporate environmental sustainability goals. According to Fairtrade International or FLO (2015), the average Fairtrade coffee plot worldwide is only 1.4 hectares (about 3.5 acres), or roughly the area of 1.3 football fields. Small farmers are encouraged to band together to form cooperatives to increase their bargaining power when selling their crop to the intermediaries between the grower and the consumer. Local middlemen called "coyotes" often pay farmers less than what it costs to produce the coffee beans. But under fair trade standards, farmers get a minimum price for their crop (the price floor), plus a price premium if the market price is above the price floor. Revenue from the premium price portion is used to support local community development (e.g., schools, public works, and environmental projects). Other goals for production under fair trade principles and standards include facilitating greater access to safe working conditions, opportunities for credit (financing) through longer term contracts with roasters and retail companies, and adopting production techniques to ensure a more environmentally friendly production process (see Dragusanu et al. 2014).

There is now a panoply of certified coffee standards. Some labeling standards focus relatively more on farmer rights while others emphasize ecological and environmental sustainability, such as reversing deforestation and protecting migratory birds. All have neutral, scientific third-party verification and/or undergo regular inspections or audits. Below I summarize the basics of some key certified fair trade coffee standards for comparison. Readers interested in finer details should consult the relevant websites.[3] Although the various standards have distinctive emphases, the aims overlap considerably. Thus, they are more alike than they differ. They represent an overlapping spectrum, with some standards more stringent, but others having a broader impact. In fact, there can be a trade-off, since the institutionalization of fair trade practices by global corporations cautiously transforms value structures. The various certifications can make it confusing for both buyers and producers.

Fairtrade, the leading and most recognized sustainable coffee certification, began in the Netherlands in the 1970s and spread to other markets. Fairtrade also certifies other products such as tea, cocoa, bananas, sugar, flowers, and cotton. In 1997, Fairtrade initiatives came together under one large umbrella called Fairtrade International (FLO), headquartered in Bonn, Germany. The Fairtrade certification mark was launched globally in 2002; it includes the word FAIRTRADE in capital letters. The heart of this certification program is a guaranteed price floor for small producers. If the market price is higher than the floor, producers receive a "social premium." Fairtrade coffee that is also organic garners a premium on top of that (about 60% of this group is organic). Additionally, Fairtrade producers are encouraged, but not required, to use more environmentally friendly pest management and other sustainable practices to prevent soil erosion and reduce water contamination.[4] The latest Fairtrade monitoring and impact report indicates that the number of farmers and plantation workers in the Fairtrade certification program (all crops and products) was more than 1.65 million in 2014; about half of this was coffee farmers (812,500) planting on 1.1 million hectares in 30 countries.

Eighty percent of this Fairtrade coffee comes from Latin America and the Caribbean (FLO 2015).

Coffee is a labor- and resource-intensive crop to grow. The movement to plant "shade-grown" coffee, for example, is a response to ecological concerns. The motivation for replacing sun-grown with shade-grown coffee is to retain forest cover, promote native flora and fauna, and provide a home for migratory birds—"biodiversity protection." Trees take carbon dioxide out of the atmosphere. (Technically, a coffee plant is a bush or a shrub, but it can grow up to 30 ft tall.) On a coffee plantation, tree roots help prevent soil and water erosion and add nutrients to the soil. Some other certifications center on coffee's water footprint and conservation of fresh water throughout the supply chain. These concerns have generated a somewhat confusing myriad of certifications sponsored by various organizations. The stringency and criteria range in strength. And many companies blend fair trade beans with conventional coffee beans so that they can claim the label even though only a percentage meets the sustainability standard. Besides Fairtrade, other major global certifications include the following:

- *Organic* certification (from the United States Department of Agriculture) prohibits the use of artificially produced agrochemicals. The market rewards 100% organic coffee with a premium price. Although it is not a requirement for organic coffee to be shade grown, it usually is.
- *Rainforest Alliance Certified*™ (RA) began in 1992 as a coalition of NGOs in Latin American called the Sustainable Agricultural Network (SAN). This certification requires shade-grown coffee (with strict numbers of different native species of shade trees per hectare to mimic a natural forest), but does not require it to be certified organic.
- *UTZ Certified* began as a Guatemalan initiative in 1997, and Utz Kapeh became an independent NGO in 2000. Its mission is to achieve sustainable agricultural supply chains in the production of coffee while at the same time embracing the FLO measures to secure economic and social benefits for farmers. The first farms were certified in 2001. Utz Kapeh (which means "good coffee" in Mayan) changed its name to UTZ Certified in 2008.
- *Smithsonian Migratory Bird Center Bird Friendly*® coffee was founded in 1997 by the Smithsonian Institution (National

Zoological Park) in Washington, DC, out of concern over the depletion of the North America migratory bird species that make their winter home in Central and South America. As a result, SMBC requires shade-grown coffee with minimum height requirements and trees per hectare, and the coffee must be organic certified.
- *4C Common Code for the Coffee Community* from the 4C Association, a membership association by the coffee industry itself (with headquarters in Bonn, Germany). The sustainability code of conduct, The Baseline Common Code, is geared primarily toward the "mainstream coffee sector." Requirements are less strict.
- *Starbucks C.A.F.E. Practices* (Coffee and Farmer Equity) collaborated in 2004 with a third-party evaluation and certification firm, SCS Global Services, to brand its own code of standards. They refer to their coffee as "ethically sourced," but only some is fair trade.

For producers/farmers to benefit from fair trade, they need to sell their harvest—a substantial portion—on fair trade terms. The firms with the highest proportion of US fair trade coffee purchases are Equal Exchange, Green Mountain Coffee Roasters, and Starbucks. There is an inverse relationship, however, between firm size and the percentage they commit to fair trade purchases. Equal Exchange, the smallest firm, buys 100% fair trade (Howard and Jaffee 2013). Since 2003, Dunkin' Donuts has sold espresso certified through Fair Trade USA and offers other blends that include fair trade coffee beans. Rainforest Alliance-certified coffee has been adopted by some large roasters and retailers such as Walmart and Kraft Foods in the USA and Lavazza in Europe. Starbucks' goal was to reach 100% "ethically sourced" fair coffee in 2015 through its own branded C.A.F.E. Practices or Fairtrade certifications; these are weaker than the requirements of Rainforest Alliance and others.

Considerable empirical research has evaluated the social and economic impact of fair trade coffee. Studies have employed careful, detailed, quantitative, qualitative, and mixed research methods. The balance of economic evidence suggests that fair trade works (Hayes 2006; Dragusanu et al. 2014). In general, farmer income has risen and plantation working conditions have improved (see, for example, Levi and Linton 2003; Kilian et al. 2004; Bacon et al. 2008; Lyon 2013; Bacon et al. 2015). Fair trade scholars Laura Raynolds and Elizabeth Bennett, in a key collection titled *Handbook of Research on Fair Trade*, term the overall impact "variegated" (2015, 21), uneven across producer groups and localities and generally falling short in reducing poverty in the developing world. My focus here is the environmental assessment of certified sustainable coffee, using the Smithsonian Bird Friendly and Rainforest Alliance certifications as focal points. Rainforest Alliance production is in the hundreds of millions of pounds, near the upper end of the certified coffee production spectrum. Smithsonian Bird Friendly is the smallest.

Two Sips: Rainforest Alliance and Smithsonian Bird Friendly Coffee

Large coffee retailers, pushed by consumers and pulled by profit, have entered the fair trade market. To capture the consumer interested in sipping a sustainable coffee, certifications have evolved to accommodate them. In the words of sociologist Daniel Jaffe from his book, *Brewing Justice*, the entrance of large corporations has unleashed "increasingly public disputes" between different segments of the movement (2007, 6). A key point of contention is granting fair trade certification to large plantations (in several crops) and whether this could hurt small farm cooperatives while mainstreaming more sustainable farming practices. This tension over the nature and extent of progressive institutional change is played out in both the Rainforest Alliance and Smithsonian Bird Friendly coffee certifications.

The Rainforest Alliance (RA) certification is broad in scope with certified shade-grown farms in 24 countries across six continents (Rainforest Alliance 2012), making it the fourth largest producer of certified coffee. According to the RA website, more than 160,000 coffee farmers globally are certified, producing on 945,000 hectares (2.3 million acres) from Central and South America, Africa, and Asia. The top producers (2012 data) are located in Brazil, Columbia, Peru, Vietnam, El Salvador and Guatemala (Potts et al. 2014, 174). Rainforest Alliance coffee certification is a standard set and managed jointly by the Rainforest Alliance and the Sustainable Agriculture Network (SAN), a group of Latin American partner organizations. A separate body, Sustainable Farm Certification International, makes the certification decisions by evaluating the audits conducted by accredited inspection bodies. Rainforest Alliance standards are based on integrated pest management (IPM) that allows for some uses of synthetic agrochemicals and thus differs from the organic certification. These standards also make some provision for protecting the rights and welfare of workers and communities. RA certification has generated controversy in the fair trade work for its emphasis on large- and medium-sized coffee plantations to accommodate the multi-nationals and because it requires farmers to reduce, but not eliminate, pesticides. Further, RA only requires plantation owners to pay farmers the relevant national minimum wage, not a living wage (Jaffee 2007, 161–162).

Production (supply) and sales (demand) of RA-certified coffee are both experiencing rapid growth. The quantity of RA-certified coffee has increased rapidly at 50% per year in recent years. Some of the largest global corporations have partnered with RA. The largest coffee company in the world, Nestlé, began working with RA in 2003. An agreement between the corporation and the NGO in 2009 to certify 80% of its Nespresso brand is from sustainable farms under the RA certification by 2013 contributed to RA's expansion. However, the branding is under Nespresso's own logo as "ecolaboration," part of their AAA Sustainable Quality™ Program. Another Nestlé brand, Nescafé instant coffee, announced an agreement to work with RA in 2010. While Nestlé is the leading global coffee company, the single largest buyer of RA-certified coffee beans is Maxwell House, a brand from Kraft Foods. McDonalds' website (McDonalds n.d.) asserts that 37% of their global coffee purchases in 2015 are from RA-certified farms; RA also supplies Taco Bell. With such widespread arrangements with large corporations, Rainforest Alliance has emerged as a Goliath in the market for certified coffee beans.

If RA produces millions of pounds of certified sustainable coffee per year, SMBC Bird Friendly Coffee is very small in scale, at less than 10 million pounds per year (9.7 million pounds in 2010, according to "The Global Market for Bird-Friendly™ Coffee: 2010" from the SMBC). But the bird-friendly shade-grown coffee has the strictest sustainability standards. Five countries account for over 90% of production: Guatemala, Peru, Mexico, Nicaragua, and Columbia.

SMBC pioneered the certification of shade coffee as distinct from organic certification to provide farmers an economic incentive to protect their plots as well as to redress the "bird-coffee connection," the destruction of a forest habitat in the tropics for North American songbirds (Jaffee 2007, 135–136). It is the only bird-friendly and organic-certified coffee, and available to small cooperatives and estate farms. A price premium is paid for bird friendly on top of the premium for the organic coffee, negotiated in long-term contracts. SMBC argues its practices lead to "better-tasting coffee" while supporting family farms and communities (SMBC n.d.). The majority of bird-friendly coffee is consumed in the USA, followed by Japan and Canada, mostly through specialty or boutique importers. In the USA, the strongest market is in the Pacific Northwest, and the supermarket chain named Fred Meyer.

Some scientific research and fieldwork on the impact of bird-friendly coffee is summarized on the SMBC blog; however, given the smaller scope of their efforts, the quantity and availability of research is much less than about RA coffee. In their first global audit, Rainforest Alliance declares it is meeting its objectives. About 70% of certified coffee farm operations conformed to the diversified shade canopy requirements and conformance has increased further over time. In addition, the certification system was effective at promoting the maintenance or establishment of protective buffer zones along the banks of rivers, streams, lakes, wetlands, and other natural water bodies, with the large majority of initial non-conformities being resolved by the most recent audit (Milder and Newsom 2015). Empirical work by scientists and environmental scholars has shown positive impacts on the environment, including water conservation, less soil erosion, reduced use of pesticides and other toxic chemicals, and a hospitable environment for migratory birds. And the impact of fair trade farming practices has been reaching conventional coffee plantations, too.

For example, Nicaraguan-certified sustainable coffee farmers have implemented more soil and water conversation practices than conventional coffee farmers (Bacon et al. 2008). Mexico's shade-grown coffee has been beneficial to water resources (Jaffee 2009; Lin 2010). In Latin America and the Caribbean, three environmental impacts were studied as a result of fair trade coffee, with positive results: biodiversity conservation, pollution reduction, and climate change adaptation (Bacon et al. 2015). In an extensive report from the Sustainable Agricultural Network (SAN) based on more than 20 research studies as well as performance and practice adoption data from 540 audit reports, Milder and Newsom (2015) find that Rainforest Alliance-certified sustainable farms across the globe apply more sustainable farm practices than non-certified farms. Important, too, are the positive externalities for conventional coffee farms:

> Certification processes are generating spillover effects on adjacent farms and communities through emulation of practices and improved transparency and traceability. Environmentally friendly technologies, such as

low-water depulping and manual, physical or biological control of pests and diseases, have reached certified farmers and extended to non-certified ones. (Milder and Newsom 2015, 39)

These findings are encouraging. They indicate that the coffee certification movement has become more than a niche market for conscious consumers. Fair trade is having a meaningful impact on agricultural practices, transforming traditional habits.

Is Fair Trade Coffee Market-Driven Social Justice?

The genie is out of the cup. The coffee market is a representative example of changes in an institutional value structure on a global scale. Sustainability, as a new value structure, has two dimensions: (1) the preservation and replenishment of natural resources and the environment, and (2) the reproduction of human society by providing the social infrastructure for the flourishing of the next generation. The movement for fair trade coffee has promoted both forms of sustainable economic development. In the subtitle of his book on fair trade coffee, Gavin Fridell (2007) calls fair trade "market-driven social justice." Fridell argues that "the global economy cannot and will not bring developmental benefits to the world's poor unless strategies are pursued which seek to counter or combat neoliberal policies and place the enhancement of human life, not merely economic growth, at the centre of development" (2007, 277). He calls fair trade one of these strategies, an organized movement for economic and social justice. And coffee is only one product. The fair trade movement itself is helping to educate consumers and apply pressure to retailers to bring more fair trade products to the marketplace.

One of the primary tactics of fair trade activists involves the certification of products and dissemination of identifiable logos. There is a long history of such activism or political consumerism in the United States (and other countries). Using product labeling to raise awareness of production processes that undermine progressive social values is one tactic (see Glickman 2009; Brown 2013). As in the past, alliances between organized groups of workers/producers and consumers work together to increase both the supply of and the demand for sustainably produced goods as interrelated processes. Today's fair trade activists have utilized and updated this tactic. Activists have interrogated the global supply chain for coffee and transformed it markedly with the growth of certified sustainable production. New institutions, including farmers' cooperatives to enhance bargaining power with distributors, have emerged. The efficacy of shade grown coffee has provided an alternative to agricultural practices that eroded soil, overutilized water, and decimated forest habitats.

Fair trade has its critics. There is a confusing myriad of certifications. Use of the marketplace makes it "reformist rather than revolutionary" (Micheletti et al. 2006, 297). Corporate interests have entered the fray with their own branded certifications that are less stringent. Ultimately, the standards and accountability are all voluntary and, therefore, less comprehensive than regulations. Consuming as a means of furthering sustainability is somewhat contradictory in its essence. This has led to charges that greening the economy is really "green-washing," meaning simply a nice-looking sheen that covers over fundamental problems.

Yet fair trade movements have a demonstrable impact on improving people's lives. The effect on global poverty has, as of yet, been insufficient, but food insecurity in farming communities is lower than it would otherwise be. Positive externalities for conventional producers have broadened the impact of fair trade practices beyond a fair trade label. Fair trade as a social movement also represents a conscious effort to rethink the logic of how markets work. Economists have demonstrated that fair trade production standards are not necessarily less efficient than the cost-cutting techniques of neoliberalism (Hayes 2006; Samuel et al. 2014). So-called free trade does not occur on a level playing field. By correcting power imbalances that generate "monopsony rents" for global distributers and retailers, sustainable and ethical production practices may actually improve economic outcomes.

In the neoliberal economy, business has itself become commodified. Companies are bought and sold and corporate executives move from firm to firm. This financialization of business has led to a shortening of time horizons. Generating short-term profits has become the priority, rather than the creation of what Thorstein Veblen referred to as *going concerns* (Jo and Henry 2015). Businesses (and other groups engaged in mutually beneficial collective action), if they are to be sustainable, going concerns, need to be attentive to a variety of stakeholders, not just shareholders. These broader stakeholders are concerned with the long-run sustainability of the economy and society. This requires a different way of doing business. It requires new institutional structures and values. Progressive institutional change places long-term thinking, that is, human, environmental, financial, and productive sustainability, at the center of economic processes. From coffee to tomatoes, from retail to restaurants, from marriage to higher education, from banking to GDP, social movements are reshaping economic institutions to make them consistent with such progressive values. Step by step, these stories demonstrate the viability of progressive institutional change.

Notes

1. The standards included in this measure are: Fairtrade, Rainforest Alliance, Organic, UTZ Certified, 4C Association, Starbucks Coffee and Farmer Equity Practices (C.A.F.E.), and Nespresso AAA Sustainable Quality.
2. Editors of one of the first books on "political consumerism" describe consumer behavior another way: "The ideal-type Egoistic Economic Man must be modified to an ideal-type Responsibility-Taking Political Consumer, who applies values other than purely self-interested ones in consumer choice situations" (Micheletti et al. 2006, xiv). Political consumerism is: "the use of market purchases by individuals, groups, and institutions who want to take responsibility for political, economic, and societal developments" (Micheletti et al. 2006, xxv).
3. The chapter references contain the website addresses of the organizations and the links to their standards. For convenience and style, as long as I am talking about the movement collectively and not a specific certification with its own label, I use the term fair trade; note the two words are in lower case lettering.
4. Fairtrade International split into two independent organizations in 2004. FLO sets Fairtrade standards and provides support to producers and FLO-CERT inspects and certifies producer organizations and audits traders. *Fair Trade USA*, a non-profit organization in the U.S. launched its own label in 2012; the U.S. organization recognizes the FLO certification and principles, but sought to certify products from larger producers and plantations. The label says "Fair Trade Certified," with three words and a capital F and T.

Supplementary Applications

1. Name some products by brand name that you have seen sold with fair trade logos such as cocoa (chocolate), coffee, tea, wine, T-shirts made from fair trade cotton, bananas, soap, cocoa butter,

shampoo, make-up, bath oil. Do you purchase any fair trade products? If so, why do you make that consumption choice?
2. Where is the closest place you can purchase a cup of fair trade coffee? What is the fair trade certification system (logo)?
3. Is there fair trade coffee at your college or university? Learn about fair trade campaigns at schools, universities, religious congregations, and towns at http://fairtradecampaigns.org/campaign-type/universities/.

REFERENCES

Altieri, Miguel A. 2009. Agroecology, Small Farms, and Food Sovereignty. *Monthly Review* 61 (3): 102–113.

Bacon, Christopher M., V. Ernesto Mendez, Maria Eugenia Flores Gomez, Douglas Stuart, and Sandro Raul Diaz Flores. 2008. Are Sustainable Coffee Certifications Enough to Secure Farmer Livelihoods? The Millennium Development Goals and Nicaragua's Fair Trade Cooperatives, *Globalizations* 5 (2): 259–274.

Bacon, Christopher M., Robert A. Rice, and Hannah Maryanski. 2015. Fair Trade Coffee and Environmental Sustainability in Latin America. In *Handbook of Research on Fair Trade*, ed. Laura T. Raynolds and Elizabeth A. Bennett, 389–404. Cheltenham: Edward Elgar.

Brown, Keith R., and Buying into Fair Trade. 2013. *Culture, Morality, and Consumption*. New York: New York University Press.

Dietsch, Thomas V., and Stacy M. Philpott. 2008. Linking Consumers to Sustainability: Incorporating Science into Eco-friendly Certification. *Globalizations* 5 (2): 247–258.

Dragusanu, Raluca, Daniele Giovannucci, and Nathan Nunn. 2014. The Economics of Fair Trade. *Journal of Economic Perspectives* 28 (3): 217–236.

Fairtrade International (FLO). Standards. http://www.fairtrade.net/standards.html.

Fairtrade International (FLO). 2015. *Scope and Benefits of Fairtrade*, 7th ed. Bonn: FLO.

Fridell, Gavin. 2007. *Fair Trade Coffee: The Prospects and Pitfalls of Market-Driven Social Justice*. Toronto: University of Toronto Press.

Galbraith, John Kenneth. 1958. *The Affluent Society*. Boston, MA: Houghton Mifflin.

Glickman, Lawrence B., and Buying Power. 2009. *A History of Consumer Activism in America*. Chicago: University of Chicago Press.

Global Coffee Platform/4C Association. Global Reference. http://www.globalcoffeeplatform.org/baseline-common-code/global-reference.

Hayes, Mark. 2006. On the Efficiency of Fair Trade. *Review of Social Economy* 64 (4): 447–468.

Howard, Philip, and Daniel Jaffee. 2013. Tensions Between Firm Size and Sustainability Goals: Fair Trade Coffee in the United States. *Sustainability* 5 (1): 72–89.

Jaffee, Daniel. 2007. *Brewing Justice: Fair Trade Coffee, Sustainability, and Survival.* Berkeley: University of California Press.

Jaffee, Daniel. 2009. 'Better, but Not Great': The Social and Environmental Benefits and Limitations of Fair Trade for Indigenous Coffee Producers in Oaxaca, Mexico. In *The Impact of Fair Trade*, ed. Ruerd Ruben, 195–222. Wageningen: Wageningen Academic Publishers.

Jo, Tae-Hee, and John F. Henry. 2015. The Business Enterprise in the Age of Money Manager Capitalism. *Journal of Economic Issues* 49 (1): 23–46.

Kilian, Bernard, Lawrence Pratt, Connie Jones, and Andrés Villalobos. 2004. Can the Private Sector be Competitive and Contribute to Development Through Sustainable Agricultural Business? A Case Study of Coffee in Latin America. *International Food and Agribusiness Management Review* 7 (3): 21–45.

Levi, Margaret, and April Linton. 2003. Fair Trade: A Cup at a Time? *Politics & Society* 31 (3): 407–432.

Lin, Brenda B. 2010. The Role of Agroforestry in Reducing Water Loss Through Soil Evaporation and Crop Transpiration in Coffee Agroecosystems. *Agricultural and Forest Meteorology* 150: 510–518.

Lyon, Sarah. 2013. *Coffee and Community.* Boulder: University of Colorado Press.

McDonald's. McDonald's and Coffee Sustainability. http://corporate.mcdonalds.com/mcd/sustainability/signature_programs/coffee_story.html.

Messier, John D. 2010. The Economics of Fair Trade. In *21st Century Economics: A Reference Handbook*, ed. Rhona Free, 503–511. Thousand Oaks, CA: Sage.

Micheletti, Michele, Andreas Follesdal, and Dietlind Stolle (eds.). 2006. *Politics, Products, and Markets: Exploring Political Consumerism Past and Present.* New Brunswick, NJ: Transaction Publishers.

Milder, Jeffrey C., and Deanna Newsom. 2015. *SAN/Rainforest Alliance Impacts Report 2015: Evaluating the Effects of the SAN/Rainforest Alliance Certification System on Farms, People, and the Environment.* New York: Rainforest Alliance and Mexico, DF: SAN.

Pay, Ellen. 2009. *The Market for Organic and Fair-Trade Coffee.* Rome: Food and Agricultural Organization (FAO).

Petty, Jules. 2009. Can Ecological Agriculture Feed Nine Billion People? *Monthly Review* 61 (6): 46–58.

Pierrot, Joost, Daniele Giovannucci, and Alexander Kasterine. 2011. Trends in the Trade of Certified Coffees. International Trade Centre (ITC) Technical Paper MAR-11-197.E, Geneva.

Potts, Jason, Matthew Lynch, Ann Wilkings, Gabriel Huppé, Maxine Cunningham, and Vivek Voora. 2014. *The State of Sustainability Initiatives Review 2014: Standards and the Green Economy*. Manitoba: International Institute for Sustainable Development (IISI) and London: International Institute for Environment and Development.

Rainforest Alliance. What Does Rainforest Alliance Certified™ Mean? http://www.rainforest-alliance.org/faqs/what-does-rainforest-alliance-certified-mean.

Rainforest Alliance. 2012. *Protecting Our Planet: Redesigning Land-use and Business Practices: 25 Years of Impacts*. New York: Rainforest Alliance.

Raynolds, Laura T., and Elizabeth A. Bennett (eds.). 2015. *Handbook of Research on Fair Trade*. Cheltenham: Edward Elgar.

Samuel, Andrew, Fred W. Derrick, and Charles Scott. 2014. 'Fair Trade', Market Failures, and (the Absence of) Institutions. *Review of Social Economy* 72 (2): 209–232.

Smithsonian Migratory Bird Center (SMBC). Bird Friendly Coffee. https://nationalzoo.si.edu/scbi/migratorybirds/coffee/.

Smithsonian Migratory Bird Center (SMBC). The Global Market for Bird-Friendly™ Coffee: 2010. https://nationalzoo.si.edu/scbi/migratorybirds/coffee/bird_friendly/global_market.cfm.

Söderbaum, Peter. 2000. Business Companies, Institutional Change, and Ecological Sustainability. *Journal of Economic Issues* 34 (2): 435–443.

Starbucks C.A.F.E. Practices. https://www.scsglobalservices.com/starbucks-cafe-practices.

United Nations Sustainable Development. 1992. Agenda 21. In *United Nations Conference on Environment & Development*. Rio de Janiero, Brazil, June 3 to 12. https://sustainabledevelopment.un.org/content/documents/Agenda21.pdf.

United States Department of Agriculture. National Organic Program. https://www.ams.usda.gov/about-ams/programs-offices/national-organic-program.

UTZ. The UTZ Standard. https://www.utz.org/what-we-offer/certification/the-standard/.

World Fair Trade Organization (WFTO). Definition of Fair Trade. http://wfto.com/fair-trade/definition-fair-trade.

Index

A
Abercrombie & Fitch, 44, 49
Affordable Care Act (ACA aka Obamacare), 74
Agricultural workers, 9, 124
Allentown, Pennsylvania, 31
Alperovitz, Gar, 76
American Civil Liberties Union (ACLU), 102
American Society of Civil Engineers (ASCE), 27, 28
American Time Use Survey (ATUS), 16, 18, 20–23
Association for Evolutionary Economics (AFEE), 2
Athleta, 44
Australia, 19–22

B
Baehr v. Lewin, 101–103
Banana Republic, 44, 49
Bank of North Dakota (BND), 29, 30
Bonauto, Mary, 101, 102, 104
Boycotts, 65, 74
Brazil, 117, 122

Brown, Ellen, 30, 91
Burger King, 64
Bush, Paul Dale, 3, 4, 6
Buycotts, 77

C
California, 31, 50, 60, 61, 65, 93, 101, 104–106
Canada, 19, 22, 45, 108, 124
Care work, 10
Chavez, Cesar, 60, 65, 69
Chicago, Illinois, 32
China, 19, 22, 61
Chipotle, 64
Climate change, 116, 124
Coalition of Immokalee Workers (CIW), 8, 61–66
Coffee certification, 115, 119, 122, 125
Coffee, trade volume, 9, 113
Colorado, 31, 103
Colors Restaurant & Bar, 8, 69
Columbia, 109, 122, 123
Committee on National Statistics (CNSTAT), 20

Commons, John R., 2, 3
Connecticut, 50, 106
Conscious consumption. *See* Ethical consumption
Consumer Finance Protection Bureau (CFPB), 82, 93
Contingent work, 47
Cooperative, 8, 66, 70, 75, 76
Corinthian Fifteen, 82

D

Darden Restaurant Group, 73
The Debt Collective, 89, 92
Debt resistance, 9, 82
Debt strike. *See* Debt resistance
Defense of Marriage Act (DOMA), 100–107
Deforestation, 116, 119
Dēmos, 31, 34, 35
Denmark, 19
Detroit, Michigan, 75
Don't Ask, Don't Tell (DADT), 104

E

Earth Summit. *See* Rio de Janeiro, Brazil, Earth Summit
East Oakland, California, 75
Economic development, 3, 7, 27–29, 31–36, 38, 76, 117, 125
El Salvador, 122
Environmental mainstreaming, 117, 122
Environmental sustainability. *See* Sustainability
Erractic work schedules. *See* Irregular work schedules
Ethical consumption, 60, 77, 114
European Union (EU), 20, 114

F

Fair Food Agreement, 8, 64, 65
Fair Labor Standards Act (FLSA), 47, 48
Fairtrade, 119–121
Fair trade coffee, impact, 121
Fair trade, defined, 114
Fair Trade International (FLO), 118–120
Farm labor. *See* Agricultural workers
Federal Deposit Insurance Corporation (FDIC), 31, 32, 34
Figart, Deborah M., 16
Financial crisis, 30, 33, 90
Finland, 19, 22
Flexibility, 43, 45, 46, 48, 53
Florida, 8, 60–63, 65
Folbre, Nancy, 6, 17, 20, 21
Food chains movie, 60
Food security, 117
4C Common Code for the Coffee Community, 121
Freedom to Marry, 100, 106

G

Galbraith, John Kenneth, 28
Gallup polling, 106
The Gap, 8, 38, 44
Gay & Lesbian Advocates and Defenders (GLAD), 102, 104
Gay marriage, state legislation, 101, 103, 106, 109
Gay rights movement, history, 102
Germany, 19, 119
GI Bill. *See* Servicemen's Readjustment Act of 1944
Gig economy, 10, 43, 45, 66
Golden, Lonnie, 46
Goodridge v. Department of Public Health, 101
Great recession, 8

Guaranteed Student Loan (GSL). *See* Stafford loan
Guatemala, 61, 122, 123

H
Haiti, 61
Harassment, 72, 73
Hardmeyer, Eric, 33
Hawaii, 31, 101–104
Higher education act of 1965, 84
"High road" employment factors, 8
Hodgson, Geoffrey, 3
Holistic pattern modeling, 7
Hotel and Restaurant Employees Union (HERE), 71
Household production, 17, 19, 22
Housework. *See* Household production
Human Rights Campaign (HRC), 104, 111

I
Identity, 2, 77, 104
Individious distinction(s), 6, 7, 9, 10, 16, 53, 87, 100, 108, 110
Infrastructure, 7, 27, 28, 34, 94
Institutional change. *See* Progressive institutional change
Institutions, defined, 3
Intemic, 44
International Coffee Agreement (ICA), 116
Irregular work schedules, 43

J
Japan, 22, 114, 124
Jayaraman, Saru, 71, 73
JCPenney, 44
J. Crew, 44

Jobs with justice, 52, 72, 92
"Just in time" scheduling, 45, 50

K
Kalleberg, Arne, 45
Kaplan, Roberta, 102, 109
Kennedy, Anthony, 100, 108
King, Coretta Scott, 105
Korea [South], 22
Kyrk, Hazel, 17

L
Lambda Legal Defense and Education Fund, 102, 104, 109
Lambert, Susan, 45, 50
Lawrence v. Texas, 103
League of women voters, 35
Luce, Stephanie, 49

M
Maine, 21, 31, 65, 107
Massachusetts, 21, 31, 35, 50, 101, 105, 106
McCrate, Elaine, 47
Mexico, 61, 62, 66, 123, 124
Minimum wage, 48, 52, 62, 72–74, 93, 123
  for tipped workers, 74
Minneapolis, Minnesota, 32
Montana, 31

N
National Academy of Sciences (NAS), 20
National Income and Product Accounts, 16, 17
National Partnership for Women & Families, 52

National Restaurant Association, 73
Neoliberal era, 9, 30, 37, 38, 43, 83, 85, 115
The Netherlands, 104, 114, 119
New Hampshire, 50
New Jersey, 50, 65, 71
New Orleans, Louisiana, 75
New York, 31, 44, 46, 48, 50–52
New York City, 46, 48, 66, 72–74, 102
New Zealand, 18, 22, 81
Nicaragua, 123
Nonpartisan League (NPL), 32
North Dakota, 7, 29, 30, 32, 33
North, Douglass, 4
Norway, 19, 22

O
Obama, Barak, 104, 105, 107
Obergefell v. Hodges, 9, 100–102, 109
Occupy student debt, 90
Occupy wall street, 9, 82, 89, 91, 94
Old Navy, 44
"On call" shifts, 8, 49–52
Oregon, 31, 50
Organic coffee, 120, 123
Oxfam, 66

P
Parent Loan for Undergraduate Students (PLUS), 85
Partnership in Assisting Community Expansion (PACE), 33
Pell grant, 84, 85
Peru, 122, 123
Philadelphia, Pennsylvania, 31
Piece rate work, 62
Pittsburgh, Pennsylvania, 31
Portugal, 22
Precariat, 45, 46, 53
Private good, 85

Progressive institutional change, defined, 2
Proposition 8 [California], 101, 105
Provisioning, 4–6, 9, 16, 28, 83, 94, 95
Public bank, 7, 28–31, 36, 37
Public Banking Institute (PBI), 31
Public good, 28, 34, 38
Public purpose, 83, 84, 94

R
Rainforest Alliance (RA), 115, 122
Reading, Pennsylvania, 31
Reich, Robert, 44
Reid, Margaret, 17
Restaurant Opportunities Center United (ROC), 66
Restaurants Advancing Industry Standards in Employment (RAISE), 75. *See also* "High road" employment factors
Restaurant workers, 8, 70–72, 75, 76
  occupational segregation, 77
  statistics, 10, 16, 18, 96
Retail Action Project (RAP), 48
Retail workers, 44, 46, 48, 50, 53
Rhode Island, 50
Rio de Janeiro, Brazil, Earth Summit, 117
Romer v. Evans, 103

S
San Francisco, California, 31, 52
Santa Fe, New Mexico, 66
Satellite accounts, 7, 16, 22, 24
Schedules That Work Act, 52
Schneiderman, Eric T., 45, 51
Seattle, Washington, 31
Servicemen's Readjustment Act of 1944, 84
Shade grown coffee, 126

Smithsonian Migratory Bird Center coffee (SMBC), 115, 121, 123
Social balance, 3, 28, 37, 38
Social entrepreneurship, 76
Social justice, 116, 125
Social reproduction, 17, 20
Stafford loan, 84
Starbucks, 8, 44, 121
Starbucks C.A.F.E. Practices, 121
Storytelling, 7
St. Paul, Minnesota, 32
Strike Debt, 90–92
Student loan debt
  average balance, 8, 82, 87, 88, 90, 92, 96
  burden, 8
  debt forgiveness, 94
  default rates, 8
  trends, 8, 82, 87, 90, 92
Student loans, private, 9, 35, 82, 93
Subway, 48, 64
Supermarkets, 8, 61, 63, 64
Sustainability, 5, 9, 76, 114, 115, 117, 119, 121, 123, 126
Sustainable Agriculture Network (SAN), 122
Sustainable economic development, 76, 125
Sweden, 19, 114

T
Taco Bell, 64, 123
Tacoma, Washington, 31
Target, 44, 74, 91
Texas, 65, 103
Time use, 7, 16–19, 21, 23, 24
T.J. Maxx, 44
Tool, Marc R., 4, 6
Trader Joe's, 53
Tuition and fees, 86, 87, 96

U
Underwork. *See* Irregular work schedules
United Farm Workers (UFW), 65
United Food and Commerical Workers (UFCW), 48
United Nations, 18, 19
United Nations Food and Agricultural Organization (FAO), 118
United States Student Association (USSA), 92
Unpredictable work schedules. *See* Irregular work schedules
Urban Outfitters, 44
U.S. Bureau of Economic Analysis (BEA), 16
U.S. Bureau of Labor Statistics (BLS), 16, 46
U.S. Department of Education, 82, 86, 90, 93
U.S. Small Business Administration, 70
U.S. Supreme Court, 99, 101, 103, 108
UTZ certified coffee, 120

V
Veblen, Thorstein, 2, 3
Vermont, 7, 31, 34–38
Vermont Economic Development Association (VEDA), 36
Vermonters for a New Economy, 35
[Vermont] Local Investment Advisory Committee (LIAC), 36
Victoria's secret, 44
Vietnam, 122

W
Wage theft, 48, 50, 73
Walmart, 45, 61, 65, 72, 121

Waring, Marilyn, 18, 19
Washington, DC, 50, 52
Washington State, 31
Wendy's, 64
Whole foods, 64
William-Sonoma, 44
Windsor, Edie, 108
Windsor v. United States, 100, 101, 107
Wolfson, Evan, 100, 102, 106

Work schedules, 8, 43, 47–49, 51–53
Working conditions, 8, 60, 66
World Bank, 34, 116
World Fair Trade Organization, 114

Z

Zara, 8, 44, 49

CPSIA information can be obtained
at www.ICGtesting.com
Printed in the USA
LVHW020547081221
705583LV00002B/224